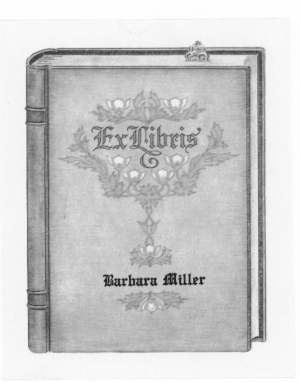

By Joseph P. McKenna

ST. LOUIS UNIVERSITY

Holt, Rinehart and Winston
New York - Chicago - San Francisco
Toronto - London

Aggregate

Economic

Analysis

Preface

KEYNES's *General Theory* has vastly altered the economic analysis of this generation. It has approached large pressing areas of economic policy with a set of tools which were simple enough for easy manipulation and which made it possible to reach reasonably meaningful empirical results. At its initial appearance, the acceptance of the analysis was involved with the acceptance of Keynes's own suggestions for policy. But now that the smoke has cleared, it appears that the general outline of the analysis has been accepted, even by those who oppose the policy conclusions, and that the amendments can be fitted into the over-all pattern.

This system has been largely hidden from students, and it has been discovered by their teachers only with difficulty. The *General Theory* itself has the distinction of being the only economics treatise provided with a key (Alvin Hansen's *Guide to Keynes*), thereby ranking with such masterpieces of obscurity as *Finnegans Wake*. Most of the later analytical articles have been polemics, designed to convince economists, not to educate students. The policy discussions have been concerned with applications and have not explained the analytical background.

The purpose of this volume is to provide a simple but carefully constructed bridge between the principles texts and the journals. It assumes no specific knowledge, though some familiarity with the ways of economists is useful. Its goal is to enable the student to discuss current policy problems and to understand the leading analytical debates. This book is intended for students, not for my colleagues. I have therefore omitted footnotes and minor quibbles. I have retained elements of controversy and indicated the ways in which policy decisions may hinge upon factual research and value judgements. The analytical structure has been clearly stated rather than merely implied in the course of an argument.

The principal innovations are pedagogical. Much of aggregate economics has traditionally been stated in algebraic terms. I have translated these into numerical examples and into the graphic tools which are more traditional to economics. Although the principal formulation follows J. R. Hicks, the devices for its derivation are novel, and even my colleagues may find uses for them. Algebraic techniques make it difficult to consider various assumptions about the shape of component functions; these grapic devices facilitate such consideration.

This is not a textbook in fiscal policy or in the history of economic thought. Most problems in fiscal policy appear somewhere, but always as illustrations of specific analytical techniques. There is little point in indoctrinating students in the best solution to current problems, since their main role in society will not be played for many years. It is far more important that they understand the process of finding answers. I have confined the history of economics to the bibliographical material at the end of each chapter and to Chapter 15. The most important thing about any economic tool is that it furthers our understanding of our society; to whom we owe this understanding is secondary.

The numerical examples of this volume are consistent but hypothetical. They were all chosen for ease of manipulation, not as exact representations of our society. Short of a loose-leaf volume, I know no way to provide currently reasonable examples, but most teachers will wish to discuss the current facts.

The first eleven chapters are frankly Keynesian in their general structure—that is, they concern themselves with the theory of effective demand, largely in the compartments set up by Keynes. In many cases, of course, the results of later amendments are clear—especially in Chapters 4, 9, 10, and 11. The later chapters review the supply side of the market, employing tools which have been in use for half a century. Finally, there is a chapter on previous theories, for the historically inclined and a chapter of examples, for those whose bent is policy. Either or both of these may be omitted if time is pressing, though my own preference would be to keep Chapter 16 and omit 15.

It is difficult to express adequately my indebtedness to my colleagues at the University of Minnesota. This book was inspired and greatly improved by our informal discussions on subject matter and presentation. It has also benefited from the suggestions and complaints of the students who used an earlier outline version, which was made possible by the School of Business Administration. Most valuable of all were the contributions of my wife, who typed and edited the manuscript and drew the diagrams. All these people improved the book; any remaining faults are mine.

JOSEPH P. McKENNA

University of Minnesota
March 1955

CONTENTS

LIST OF ILLUSTRATIONS

CHAPTER 1

Introduction

Economics is the study of the relation of man's wants to his resources. In the past, economics has been concerned principally with problems of choice—for example, how much labor and how much capital should be used to produce a given product. Economics has discussed many aspects of these problems of choice, but its principal focus has always been the study of individual firms and households. Most of the elementary textbooks in economics published in this century have emphasized this kind of analysis.

In recent literature, a different problem has become more prominent. The theory of choice emphasizes the *direction* of expenditure or of resource use but is little concerned with the question of *whether* the expenditure will be made at all or the resource used. This narrowness of focus stemmed from the belief that in the long run all income would be spent (either for consumption or for investment) and all resources employed. Consideration of the justification for such belief is beyond the scope of this book. However, it is now abundantly clear that in the short run, at least, income can be saved and not invested, and resources can be unemployed. It is therefore of interest to us to consider what factors determine the short-run levels of demand and supply of total production. We shall then be in a position to discuss the level of national income, the level of prices, and the level of employment.

Before continuing, let us consider precisely what problems we hope to solve. We have said that we wish to consider total production. We might do this in at least two ways.

The first method seems perfectly straightforward. If we want to consider total production, we need only consider in turn every firm and household and their outputs. Then, if we understand each of these, we shall understand total production, just as one might come to "understand" a forest by examining the plants and animals which compose it. However, the sheer magnitude of the task indicates that before we finished studying the last household, any information gleaned about the first would be obsolete. But even this understates the difficulty of the task, for it is not possible to study the elements one by one. Each unit (firm or household) is affected by other units—if not all other units, at least those near by—as the tree in the forest is affected by those around it. In order to accomplish the task that we have outlined, it would be necessary to consider millions of households and thousands of firms at the same time. This task is beyond the capabilities not only of a man with pencil and paper but also of any computing machine now in existence.

The second method is more modest. It suggests that we

throw away some information, thereby getting the problem down to a manageable size. Instead of considering the income of each household, we might lump all these household incomes together and discuss national income. We shall consider this total in more detail in Chapter 2.

For the moment, let us remind ourselves of the questions we cannot hope to answer in this fashion. Since by this method we shall be considering only total income, we can learn nothing about why incomes are distributed in a certain way. Since we shall consider all commodities together, we can say nothing about the relative quantities of margarine and butter sold. Many similar problems will go unanswered for the same reason. The one advantage in this method is that it enables us to discuss the totals, whereas if we insist on the complete survey called for by the first method, we may find our aspirations nobler but our accomplishments fewer.

It must not be supposed that the problems and methods discussed in this book comprise all of modern economics. Our treatment here of the selected topics constitutes little more than an introduction and leaves much to the student's future work. In particular, changes over time are discussed only briefly. Nor are the problems selected for discussion here the only important ones. The theory of choice still offers the only method of understanding many of the problems omitted and is still an important part of economics. We are here considering only an approximation method, which is adequate for some purposes. Beyond this limited scope, no claims should be made.

The discussion that comprises this book is a single unit. We could "lay out" the entire system at the outset and spend the remainder of the book justifying each part. Instead, we shall study each topic separately, adding it to the material that has gone before. In this way, we shall use the intermediate steps to build the total system.

Like many problems in economics, aggregate analysis can be divided into the study of supply and the study of demand. Chapters 3 through 11 discuss demand, first in its simplest form and then gradually broadening the view to a summary of the entire market for goods and services and its relation to the money market. All these discussions assume fixed prices—that is, they explain *shifts* in the demand curve but not *movements* along it. Chapter 11 introduces price variation and movements along the demand curve. Chapters 12 through 14 discuss aggregate supply. Chapter 15 is a note on the history of economic thought and Chapter 16 an application of the analysis to certain questions of public policy.

It is not possible to give final answers to any of these policy problems. Any answer has three components: the *facts* of the real world, the *analysis* of the relation between these facts, and the *value judgments* of the decision maker. This book, by necessity, concentrates on the analysis, for the facts change quite rapidly and the value judgments vary among individuals. The economist must limit himself to the analysis of problems and their alternative solutions, leaving to philosophers the choice of the best morally acceptable solution.

In the course of our discussion, we shall often use rather simple forms of mathematical formulations. Even when the form of the discussion is verbal, many of the principles will be similar to those of mathematics, for mathematics is merely one form of logic. It will therefore be useful at this point to examine the structure of this mathematical kind of analysis.

The basis of any descriptive system is a certain number of relations, or *functions*. Function is merely a general term for a statement that tells us the value of one number if we know the value of one or more other numbers. Thus, "John is five years older than his brother Bob" is a verbal statement of a function. If we know how old Bob is, we can find John's age. This is a very simple function; many functions involve more than two numbers. "The population of New England is equal to the sum of the populations of Maine, New Hampshire, Vermont, Massachusetts, Rhode Island, and Connecticut" is a function relating the population of New England to six other figures, the populations of the individual states.

For convenience, we call the components of these functions *variables*. Thus, our first function contains two variables, John's age and Bob's age. The second contains seven variables, the population of New England and that of each of the six states. The term "variable" may be a source of some confusion, since the factors which it represents may be fixed. Thus, at the moment, John's age is a fixed number. However, we do not yet know what that number is, and we must leave our imagination free to range over various possible values. If we can obtain enough relations, we shall be able to find the one set of values that will satisfy all the functions and enable us to obtain values for all the variables.

Now the question arises as to how many relations would be "enough." If we know that John is five years older than Bob, how much more information—or "relations"—would we need in order to know John's age? It should be obvious that we need one more bit of information, which might be of various types. Either of the following will suffice.

> Bob is half John's age.
> Bob is five years old.

With either of these items of information, we could find that Bob is five and John is ten. Coming back to the population of New England, we need six additional pieces of information— that is, the population of each of the six states involved. We must, however, be careful about defining "additional" information. If John is five years older than Bob, the statement that Bob is five years younger than John is not additional information but merely the same thing we already know stated in a different form.

In the same way, if we are told the population of Maine, New Hampshire, Vermont, Massachusetts, and Rhode Island and the combined population of Maine and New Hampshire, we still cannot arrive at the population of New England, because, although we have six bits of information, only five add to our knowledge. Learning the population of Maine and New Hampshire together gives us no added information if we already know the population of the two states separately.

We can therefore state as a general rule that in order to obtain a solution to any of our problems, we must have as many *independent* functions as we have variables. A system that satisfies this requirement is called a *closed* system, whereas a system that has fewer relations than are necessary is called an *open* system.

If we wish always to obtain complete answers, we can consider only closed systems. Often, however, it is useful to consider something less than a complete answer, especially as an intermediate step to a final solution. In elementary economics, it is explained that a supply curve can be derived from a set of functions covering the costs of individual factors of production, the technical production function, and the rules of profit maximization. That system of functions is not a closed system but an open one. The supply curve merely summarizes all these other relationships into one single function relating price and quantity. Only by adding another function, the demand curve, can we actually find the price and output. Nevertheless, the supply curve is useful as a device for summarizing a number of functions. In some chapters we shall discuss open systems, leaving to later a consideration of the additional information needed to close the systems.

In times past, when the government played only a small part in the economic activities of this country, it was possible for economists to construct a closed system. However, the government now is a large purchaser of goods and services. The explanation for such increased government activity is beyond the competence of an economist, since it involves a large area of political decision.

An open system can be made into a formally closed system

simply by assigning an arbitrary function giving the value of any variable we do not wish to explain. In our first example above, our statement that Bob's age is five years may be regarded as such a function; it tells Bob's age regardless of the value of the other variables. (In mathematics, this is called a function even though it is arbitrary, for it enables us to find Bob's age if we know John's age. The fact that we know that Bob is five even if we know nothing of John's age is considered unimportant.) Often we shall represent such a value by an arbitrary symbol, to indicate that this variable has a value that we have no intention of explaining. We shall see, for example, that it is ordinarily possible to rearrange the information we have in such a way that any one of the other variables can be stated as a function of the variable that we are not explaining.

It is customary to call the variables that we do *not* intend to explain *exogenous* and those that we explain *endogenous*. The distinction between exogenous and endogenous variables is not a property of the real world but merely a description of the self-imposed limitation of our analysis. In the chapters to come, we shall start with a very simple system, adding new relations and new variables in later chapters. Often variables which have been treated as exogenous in earlier chapters will be treated as endogenous in later chapters, as our analysis becomes extended.

We shall usually designate variables by capital letters. The value of an exogenous variable will be represented by the letter for that variable with a subscript zero.

It may be useful to summarize the mathematical tools that we shall use. A function is represented by an equation which indicates the equality between two numbers or groups of numbers. An equation is unaffected by any change provided that the change is made on both sides of the equation. Thus, we can add the same number to each side, subtract the same number, multiply by the same number, or divide by the same number without changing the basic statement the equation makes. To illustrate these principles, let us use the example of the two boys' ages. We shall represent John's age by J, Bob's age by B. We then have two equations:

(1) $$J = B + 5.$$

(2) $$B = \tfrac{1}{2} J.$$

To find John's age, let us insert the value of B from the second equation into the first equation. We then have

(3) $$J = (\tfrac{1}{2} J) + 5.$$

Subtracting $\tfrac{1}{2} J$ from each side, we obtain

(4) $$J - \tfrac{1}{2} J = \tfrac{1}{2} J + 5 - \tfrac{1}{2} J.$$
$$\tfrac{1}{2} J = 5.$$

We then multiply both sides by 2:

(5) $$2(\tfrac{1}{2} J) = 2 \times 5.$$
$$J = 10.$$

To find Bob's age, we insert this value into either the first or second equations. If we use equation 1, we get

(6) $\qquad\qquad 10=B+5.$

Subtracting 5 from each side gives us

(7) $\qquad\qquad 10-5=B+5-5.$
$$5=B.$$

    For such a simple problem, these techniques may seem needlessly complicated. For later problems they will be quite useful. No more complicated mathematical tools will be required.

    Another way of solving the same problem would be to draw a graph of each of the two equations, in which case the solution is found at the intersection of the two graphs. This method is exemplified in Figure 1.

    One final problem remains. Often we group certain numbers within parentheses. When we remove the parentheses, we must multiply *each* number inside the parentheses by the number that stands in front of the parentheses. We must also watch the signs carefully. Minus times minus or plus times plus results in a plus sign; minus times plus, in a minus sign. The following examples are presented as a reminder of these rules.

(8) $\qquad\qquad 18+2(6+2)=18+12+4.$
$$18+2(8)=34.$$

(9) $\qquad\qquad 18+2(6-2)=18+12-4.$
$$18+2(4)=26.$$

(10) $\qquad\qquad 18-2(6+2)=18-12-4.$
$$18-2(8)=2.$$

(11) $$18-2(6-2)=18-12+4.$$
$$18-2(4)=10.$$

When general cases are discussed in this book, we shall use letters to represent numbers. The principles we have discussed above will nevertheless still apply.

PROBLEMS

Find values for x and, where applicable, for y.

(1) $\quad\quad\quad x=18+(3+4).$

(2) $\quad\quad\quad x=14-(4+5).$

(3) $\quad\quad\quad x=25-(8-2).$

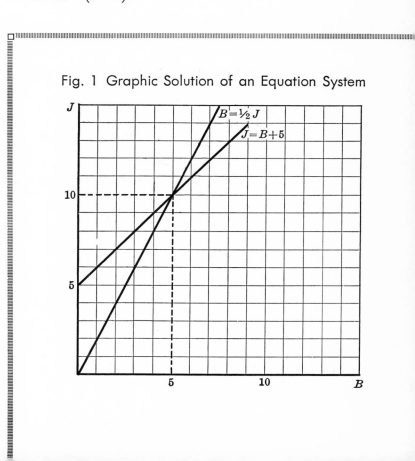

Fig. 1 Graphic Solution of an Equation System

(4) $x = 19 - 4(8-2).$
(5) $4x + 12 = 36.$
(6) $6x - 5 = 29.$
(7) $18 - 2x = 4.$
(8) $y = x + 10.$
           $y = 2x.$
(9) $y = 4x + 12.$
           $y = 9x + 2.$
(10) $4y = x + 5.$
           $x = y + 13.$
(11) $2y = x + 8.$
           $x = 3y - 14.$
(12) $y = x + 4.$
           $x = \frac{3}{4}y + 1.$

SUGGESTED ADDITIONAL READINGS

Those who are unfamiliar with the elementary mathematics discussed in this chapter will find a brief discussion in W. L. Crum and J. A. Schumpeter, *Rudimentary Mathematics for Economists and Statisticians* (New York: McGraw-Hill, 1946), Chapters 1 and 2. These chapters also contain a review of simple graphic analysis.

CHAPTER 2

National Income and Its Measurement

THE ANALYSIS presented in this book deals primarily with an explanation of changes in the various money flows of our economy. Each flow is measured as a certain number of dollars per unit of time. The first such flow is national income.

National income is the sum of the earned incomes of all individuals during a given period of time. In the United States, national income is usually measured on an annual basis. The sum thus determined must be distinguished from the total of cash receipts by individuals. Money withheld from wages is earned but not included in cash receipts. The same is true of earnings retained by corporations or of wages earned but not paid, as would be the case if the end of the year fell in the middle of a work week. Gifts, either from individuals or from the government, are cash receipts but are not earned and are therefore not considered as income.

Incomes are earned by producing goods or services. The

value of production is represented by the incomes of the producers, in the form of wages, salaries, rent, interest, or profits. Thus, the total of all incomes must be identical with the value of all goods produced, for all income is generated by production and all production generates income.

In trying to determine national income by adding up production, we must be very careful not to count any production twice. The national product does not include the total value of steel plus the total value of automobiles, for some of the steel went into the automobiles. We can therefore think of the national product as the total value of *additions* to product made by the automobile industry, the steel industry, and all others. This addition, or *value added,* includes all payments made to factors of production but excludes amounts paid to other firms. National income is thus similar to the consolidated income of a corporation and its subsidiaries.

Another way of avoiding double counting would be to total all final goods and services (those sold outside the business system) and add that part of the output of steel and other intermediate goods which is not included in the value of final products. The total of final products includes all goods and services sold to consumers, to the government, and to foreign buyers. The intermediate goods that we must add are all those that go into inventories, machinery, business construction, and the like. In this manner, we exclude all sales to businesses that go into further production but include those that add to the capital of the firm. (Readers with some background in accounting will notice that we exclude all those purchases which appear as expenses. Purchases on capital account are not considered as expenses but are included in the income of the selling firms.)

In our discussions of national income and product, we adopt a rather simplified view of firms. For our purposes, firms exist to channel funds from purchasers to producers. All funds received by each firm belong to some consumer, either the workers or the owners. It is true that some of these funds go to other firms, but that is merely an intermediate step on the way to some consumer. Defining national income as the sum of total production or earned incomes is the same as saying that national income equals the total of all receipts by firms or of all sums paid or owed by firms to consumers. We also talk as if all production moved through firms, although consumers and the government sometimes hire labor directly. This verbal fiction is adopted merely to simplify our discussion; it does not pretend to describe the behavior of our society.

Of the many statistical estimates of national income that have been made, the most valuable for historical purposes are those made by Simon Kuznets for the National Bureau of Economic Research. Current estimates are made by the Department of Commerce, using three different definitions (see pp. 22-23).

For many purposes, individuals are more interested in their receipts, or take-home pay, than in their earnings. We call these actual receipts *disposable income*. Disposable income is approximately equal to national income minus taxes plus transfer payments (gifts, pensions, etc.) from the government.

Gifts from individuals may be ignored in a consideration of national income because they subtract from the giver's disposable income what they add to the receiver's income. There are other differences between national income and disposable income (e.g., retained corporate earnings), but they need not concern us here.

THE USES AND SOURCES OF INCOME

Disposable income can be used either for consumption or for saving. Certain conceptual problems arise in the measurement of consumption. In many cases in economics, we take consumption to mean the actual using up of goods by consumers. From the standpoint of measuring economic welfare, this definition is clearly correct. An individual's economic lot is improved only by his using the goods he buys. Unfortunately, no statistics are available on the actual use of goods. The statisticians are therefore forced to measure consumption in terms of the purchase of goods by one who presumably will use them for satisfaction—that is, by a consumer. As regards services and perishable goods, the difference between goods purchased and goods consumed is very slight. In the case of durable goods, however, the difference may be great. During wartime, for example, few durable goods are purchased, but many are used for years later. For purposes of analyzing national income, it is desirable to measure consumption at the time of purchase, for it is at this time that the goods are withdrawn from the economic system and make their contribution to the incomes of the producers.

For measuring the consumption of residential housing, a

different method is used. Houses are very expensive and long-lasting. For this reason, many buyers think of them as investments. In addition, many houses are purchased by investors and made available to consumers on a rental basis. To ensure uniformity of treatment, national-income analysts regard the purchase of all houses as an investment and treat the owners as though they were renting the houses to themselves. Only the rental value is regarded as current consumption. This procedure is completely justifiable only if one believes that all home buyers behave like investors—that is, that they are motivated by the same factors. Nevertheless, it is a reasonably satisfactory approximation.

Saving is that portion of income which is not spent for consumption. It may be represented by increases in bank deposits, purchases of securities, or cash hidden in sugar bowls. If saving is negative (when consumption is greater than income), we refer to it as "dis-saving." Saving, which is a flow concept, should be distinguished from the assets that may accumulate as the result of saving. These sums are termed *savings* in ordinary parlance but will be called *assets* here.

If we examine national income in terms of products, we see that it consists of sales of final goods and services and additions to business-capital accounts. Additions to business-capital accounts are called *investment*. Sales of final goods are classified, according to the purchaser, as *consumption, government expenditures,* or *net exports.* Let us consider each briefly.

Investment consists primarily of plant and equipment sales plus additions to business inventories. All these items refer only to purchases of productive goods, not to purely financial investments. If an individual buys a stock or bond, he thinks of this purchase as an investment. From the standpoint of society as a whole, no investment has taken place, for the investment by the purchaser was matched by *dis*investment (negative investment) by the seller. Even if he purchases newly issued securities, he is merely exchanging his money for the promise of the corporation. Only when the corporation spends the money for productive purposes does investment which is not matched by disinvestment take place.

Another common form of disinvestment involves the purchase of a new plant or new equipment. As plant and equipment are used up, they tend to decline in value. Firms call this decline *depreciation* and include it as an expense. Therefore, the *net* increase in capital equipment is the value of the new investment minus the depreciation on old equipment.

The Department of Commerce uses both gross investment and net investment in measuring national product. From the standpoint of economic welfare, the net figure is more important. The gross estimates are used because they are easier to measure (depreciation is a rather imprecise figure) and because the gross product is a better indication of goods available for a short period of time. During wartime, for example, we used almost all our production for war purposes rather than for the replacement of capital goods. War mobilizers were therefore more interested in gross national product.

By *government expenditures* we mean only outlays for the purchase of goods and services. This definition follows logically from our definition of national income as earned income only, excluding other payments. For the government, these other payments are quite large. They include pensions, subsidies, relief, and unemployment compensation. As actually computed, they also include interest on the government debt. This last item is debatable, for the government receives the use of the money just as any private borrower would. The principal reason for this treatment is that the government could also obtain the money simply by printing it. It chooses to borrow money for various reasons. The interest payment is then treated as a subsidy to those who do what the government wishes (*e.g.*, who save money instead of contributing to wartime inflation). In any case, transfer payments are additions to individuals' disposable income. They are, in effect, negative taxes, for taxes are payments made by individuals to the government without direct compensation and transfers are payments by the government to individuals, again without direct compensation.

Although we shall not discuss international trade in the remainder of this book, we must mention here that net exports are also included in national income. Exported goods are a portion of total product (and income) which is not included in sales to the government, consumers, or businesses. Imports, on the other hand, are included in the purchases of these groups but not in production. Therefore, production exceeds domestic sales by the excess of exports over imports. (If imports are larger, sales exceed production.) Thus, the *net* balance of trade appears as a balancing item in national-income statistics. For the sake of simplicity, we shall ignore this item. A change in this net balance has the same effects on national income as an equal change in investment or government spending. (Statisticians may worry about whether to enter Marshall Plan aid or Lend Lease as government spending or net exports. Economists are unconcerned about the outcome since the analysis is the same in either case.)

In summary, then, from the point of view of production, we may say that national income equals consumption plus investment plus government expenditures. Income is used for consumption, saving, or taxes. However, some of the money applied to these purposes comes from transfer payments, so, from the point of view of use, national income equals consumption plus saving plus taxes minus transfers.

REAL INCOME AND MONEY INCOME

All the money flows that we have been discussing are measured in money terms. We have no choice in this measurement, for each flow represents a sum of payments for a large number of heterogeneous items. Consumption, for example, includes payments for food, clothing, rent, movies, baseball bats, and lollipops. Only the money payments involved give us a common measuring stick for these discrete items. This measuring stick has a number of disadvantages, the greatest of which is that it changes size from year to year. If we hear that national income has risen since last year, we cannot conclude that more goods and services have necessarily been produced or that the measuring stick has changed in size. The typical explanation is some combination of both, a change in production *and* a change in prices. As a device to measure the change in production, we divide the money national income by the price index. For example, national income was 40 billion dollars in 1933 and 240 billion dollars in 1950. However, prices were twice as. high in 1950, so we say that national income in 1950 was 120 billion dollars measured in 1933 dollars. Such a computation indicates that three times as many goods and services were produced in 1950 as in 1933. This bundle of goods and services is called the *real income*, whereas the money value is called *money income*.

Our measurement of real income is not a precise one; the constant addition of new products and changes in the quality of old ones makes it impossible to obtain any exact comparisons. But even the approximate figures we can obtain are better than figures which take no account of the difference between money income and real income.

ABBREVIATIONS

Throughout this book, we shall refer to the various components of national income, sometimes in mathematical form. The following abbreviations have been adopted for the sake of convenience:

$$Y = \text{Income.}$$
$$Y_D = \text{Disposable income.}$$
$$C = \text{Consumption.}$$
$$S = \text{Saving.}$$

I = Investment.

Tx = Taxes.

Tr = Transfers.

G = Government expenditures.

All are measured in money terms. When we wish to indicate real quantities, we shall use an asterisk to indicate that we have divided by a price index to correct for changes in price. Thus $Y* = \dfrac{Y}{P}$ —that is, income measured at some fixed level of prices —say, 1939.

DEPARTMENT OF COMMERCE DEFINITIONS

In the United States, the best current estimates of national income are made by the Department of Commerce and are published in the *Survey of Current Business*, especially in the supplement to the July issue. These estimates utilize three definitions: gross national product, net national product, and national income. Gross national product (*GNP*) contains no allowance for depreciation; net national product (*NNP*) does. National income measures earned incomes and differs from net national product primarily by the amount of taxes paid by business and subsidies received. Since these taxes are included in selling price but not in earned incomes, *NNP* is sometimes called "national income at market prices" and national income, "national income at factor cost." There is also a statistical discrepancy resulting from the difference in measurement of the sum of incomes and the sum of products. Table 1 presents the

1947	1948	1949	1950	1951	1952	1953	1954
165.0	177.6	180.6	194.0	208.3	218.4	230.1	234.0
29.7	41.2	32.6	51.2	56.9	50.6	51.4	46.1
28.6	36.6	43.6	42.0	62.8	77.2	85.2	77.5
8.9	2.0	0.5	−2.2	0.2	−0.2	−1.9	−0.6
232.2	**257.3**	**257.3**	**285.1**	**328.2**	**346.1**	**364.9**	**357.1**
14.1	16.5	18.4	20.5	23.5	25.3	27.2	21.3
218.1	**240.8**	**238.9**	**264.6**	**304.8**	**320.8**	**337.6**	**335.8**
18.9	20.6	21.8	23.5	25.4	28.3	30.6	30.6
0.7	0.7	0.8	0.8	1.0	1.0	1.0	1.0
1.4	−2.1	0.0	0.2	1.3	0.6	1.0	4.0
197.2	**221.6**	**216.2**	**240.0**	**277.0**	**291.0**	**305.0**	**300.2**
15.5	15.0	16.2	19.0	16.4	17.0	17.8	20.2
0.7	0.7	0.8	0.8	1.0	1.0	1.0	1.0
6.8	10.9	10.3	8.1	8.3	7.1	8.0	8.0
5.7	5.2	5.7	6.9	8.2	8.7	8.8	9.7
11.3	12.5	10.4	17.8	22.5	20.0	21.1	17.2
0.0	0.0	0.0	0.0	0.1	0.0	0.0	0.0
190.5	**208.7**	**206.8**	**227.0**	**255.3**	**271.2**	**286.1**	**286.5**
21.5	21.1	18.7	20.9	29.3	34.4	36.0	32.9
169.0	**187.6**	**188.2**	**206.1**	**226.0**	**236.8**	**250.1**	**253.6**
165.0	177.6	180.6	194.0	208.3	218.4	230.1	234.0
4.0	**10.0**	**7.6**	**12.1**	**17.7**	**18.4**	**20.0**	**19.6**

statistical data for national income of recent years and shows the relation among these various concepts.

When we use the unspecified term *national income* or the abbreviation Y, we are talking about a concept that is closest to net national product. From this we obtain disposable income by subtracting all taxes, business and personal, and adding transfers. The other differences between national income and disposable income as computed may be considered business saving.

PROBLEMS AND DISCUSSION QUESTIONS

1. If a firm manufactures materials for another firm but gives them away free, what problems would this raise in measuring national income?

2. Does paying off debts constitute saving? Why?

3. If we treated the purchase of automobiles as investment instead of as consumption, what difference would it make in the accounts in the year the automobile is purchased? in the years it is used?

4. Relief payments are treated as transfer payments; wages, as government expenditures and income. How would you classify payments made by the government to otherwise unemployed workers hired to do useless work?

5. In 1939, prices were 60 percent of the 1947 level; in 1953, they were 120 percent. Using the data of Table 1, compare the real *GNP* in these three years.

6. Which of the measures given in Table 1 do you consider the best criterion of a country's economic welfare?

SUGGESTED ADDITIONAL READINGS

The generally accepted national accounts for the United States are those prepared by the Department of Commerce. These are issued annually, usually in a supplement to the July issue of the *Survey of Current Business*. The 1954 supplement discusses in some detail the method of derivation of the estimates.

For earlier periods, the best estimates are those prepared by Simon Kuznets for the National Bureau of Economic Research, a private organization. The estimates are summarized in Kuznets, *National Income: A Summary of Findings* (1946), and details of the earlier estimates are given in Kuznets, *National Product since 1869* (1946). The problem of properly defining national income is treated thoroughly in the first three chapters of Kuznets, *National Income 1919-1938* (1941). All three books are published in New York by the National Bureau.

International comparisons of statistics are issued periodically by the United Nations. United Nations, *Measurement of National Income and the Construction of Social Accounts* (1947) defines standards for these statistics.

CHAPTER 3

The Simplest System

M ANY DISCUSSIONS of the determination of income center around a very simple explanation of the level of aggregate demand. This system uses the definition of income given in Chapter 2, which records the fact that income results from sales of goods and services to consumers, to investors, and to the government. Of these three types of sales, we shall explain only consumer purchases, designating investment and government spending as exogenous variables. In other words, we are not going to explain these last two factors but shall merely take them as given. If we were trying to arrive at a numerical estimate of national income, we should need a good crystal ball to provide the values of these two factors. The analysis of this chapter will not help us to find them but only to examine their effects.

The list of variables and the basic equations for this chapter are given below. Equation 1 gives the definition of national income; equations 3 and 4 merely designate investment and government expenditure as exogenous. Equation 2, the consumption function, is discussed below.

VARIABLES:

Endogenous

Y = National income.

C = Consumer expenditures.

Exogenous

I = Investment expenditures.

G = Government expenditures for goods and services.

EQUATIONS:

(1) $\qquad\qquad Y = C + I + G.$

(2) $\qquad\qquad C = a + bY.$

(3) $\qquad\qquad I = I_0.$

(4) $\qquad\qquad G = G_0.$

All prices are assumed to be constant.

THE CONSUMPTION FUNCTION

There are several reasons for describing consumption in the manner indicated in equation 2. It is a common observation that as an individual's income increases he usually spends a part of the increase for consumption and saves a part. Therefore, the ratio of the increase in consumption expenditure to the increase in income is ordinarily between zero and one. (We might imagine some individuals who would react in a perverse fashion, but they would not be typical.) We are not so much interested in individual behavior as in the behavior of the whole society, but the same principles that apply to individuals will apply to the society. An increase in national income will mean increases in income for some individuals. Since most of them will save some and consume some, it is reasonable to assume that the same relationship between income and consumption exists for the society as a whole. This relationship is usually designated as the *consumption function.*

Many attempts have been made statistically to find the precise form of this relationship. These studies indicate that many factors in addition to income affect the level of consumption. Such refinements are discussed in Chapter 10, together with some of the statistical results. As a first approximation, we shall ignore these other variables and discuss only the relation between income and consumption.

A few words are necessary to justify the form of relationship that we have chosen to discuss. In many cases, it would be convenient to assume that every dollar of increase in income is reflected in an equal increase in consumption—to assume, that is, that if an increase in income of $100 causes an increase of $80 in consumption, an increase in income of $1,000 would cause an increase in consumption of $800, not $750 or $900. As we shall see in Chapter 10, we have reason to believe that the real world is not quite so simple; however, if we make the assumption that the increase is proportionately the same for all levels of income and confine our discussion to a fairly narrow range of incomes, any error we make will be fairly small. Thus, if an increase in income of $100 causes an increase of $80 in consumption, we should expect an additional increase of $100 in income to cause an additional increase in consumption of about $80, although it might actually be $78 or $82. In any case, the error in assuming it to be $80 would be small.

The form of equation we have chosen (a straight line) embodies this assumption that every addition to income involves a constant addition to consumption. Let us represent an increase in consumption by ΔC and an increase in income by ΔY. If income increases from Y to $Y+\Delta Y$, consumption will increase from C to $C+\Delta C$. Using equation 2, we find that

(5)
$$C+\Delta C = a+b(Y+\Delta Y)$$
$$= a+bY+b\Delta Y.$$

Subtracting equation 2,

(6)
$$\Delta C = b\Delta Y.$$

The letter b represents the portion of *additional* income that will be consumed. This proportionality factor is called the *marginal propensity to consume*. It is called marginal because it applies only to additions to income.

We can draw a graph of the consumption function, as shown in Figure 2. The marginal propensity to consume can be measured by drawing a triangle with sides parallel to the axes (base lines), using the consumption function as the hypotenuse. The marginal propensity to consume is then the ratio of ΔC to ΔY. For the straight-line equation which we have chosen, it is apparent that this ratio is the same regardless of the size and position of the triangle.

We might also, on occasion, be interested in the average propensity to consume, or the proportion of the average dollar which is consumed—that is, the ratio of C to Y. In Figure 2, we represent this ratio by drawing a line to the zero point, then using this line as the hypotenuse of a triangle. We can then measure C parallel to the vertical axis and Y along the horizontal axis. For the equation we have chosen, this ratio, unlike the

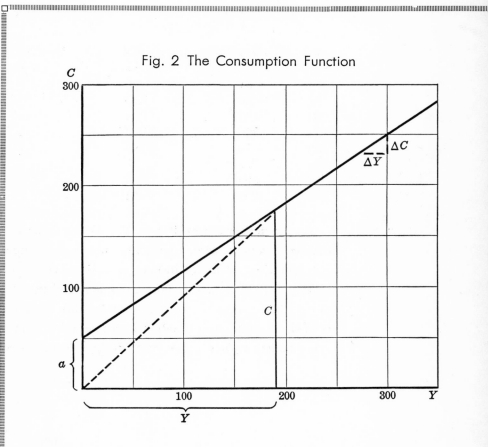

Fig. 2 The Consumption Function

marginal propensity, is not a constant but is different at every level of income. When income is low, the ratio will be more than one, indicating that people spend more than their incomes for consumption. At high incomes, the average propensity is smaller, indicating that people do not spend all their incomes but instead save some. Table 2 gives a hypothetical value of the consumption function and the average and marginal propensities to consume.

TABLE 2

HYPOTHETICAL CONSUMPTION FUNCTION
(Unit: one billion dollars)

Income	Consumption	Average Propensity to Consume	Marginal Propensity to Consume
$ 0	$ 50		.67
60	90	1.50	.67
120	130	1.08	.67
150	150	1.00	.67
180	170	.94	.67
240	210	.88	.67
300	250	.83	.67
360	290	.81	.67

As can be seen from Figure 2, *a* is the value of consumption when income is zero. Using the numerical example of Table 2, *a* is 50 billion dollars. However, one should not attach especial importance to this factor. Our argument for using a straight line was that it would give us a reasonably accurate description of the consumption function in the neighborhood of equilibrium income. Clearly, the zero income level is not in that neighborhood. Therefore, a should be regarded as the constant that determines the level of the consumption function and b as the constant that determines its slope. An increase in a means that the whole line moves upward parallel to its present position; an increase in b means that the line becomes steeper.

EQUILIBRIUM INCOME

We are now prepared to consider the solution to this system of equations, to find the level of national income that will satisfy these conditions. We call such a level the *equilibrium* income, since there would be no tendency to move from this position, once it is attained, unless conditions change. We are not explaining the level of investment or of government spending; therefore, the most we can hope for is a formal solution that illustrates the dependence of the equilibrium income upon these factors. To find such a solution, let us recall the definition of equation 1:

(1) $$Y = C + I + G.$$

We now substitute in the right-hand side of this equation the values of C, I, and G given by equations 2, 3, and 4, respectively. We then obtain

(7) $$Y = (a + bY) + I_0 + G_0.$$

Subtracting bY from both sides,

(8) $$Y - bY = a + I_0 + G_0.$$

We now divide by $(1-b)$ and obtain

(9) $$Y = \frac{1}{1-b}(a+I_0+G_0).$$

This solution tells us the level of national income that we could expect if we knew I_0 and G_0 and had the numerical values of a and b. For those who prefer arithmetical solutions, this technique is indicated in Table 3. We have used the consumption function of Table 2 and assumed I_0 to be 30 billion dollars and G_0 to be 20 billion dollars.

TABLE 3

HYPOTHETICAL INCOME DATA
(Unit: one billion dollars)

Y	C	I_0	G_0	$C+I_0+G_0$
0	50	30	20	100
60	90	30	20	140
120	130	30	20	180
150	150	30	20	200
180	170	30	20	220
240	210	30	20	260
300	250	30	20	300
360	290	30	20	340

In Table 3, the equilibrium level is 300. Only at this level would the sum of investment plus government spending plus the consumption appropriate to that level add up to the total of national income.

A graphic illustration of this solution technique is presented in Figure 3. We have here taken the graph of the consumption

function shown in Figure 2 and added to it the level of investment and of government spending, which corresponds to the last
column of Table 3. The equilibrium value is located at the
point at which the sum of all these expenditures is equal to the
income. Since the income is measured on the horizontal scale
and all these expenditures are measured on the vertical scale,
it is useful to extend income vertically. This is done by adding a
line at a 45-degree angle upward, the $Y=Y$ line. The equilib-

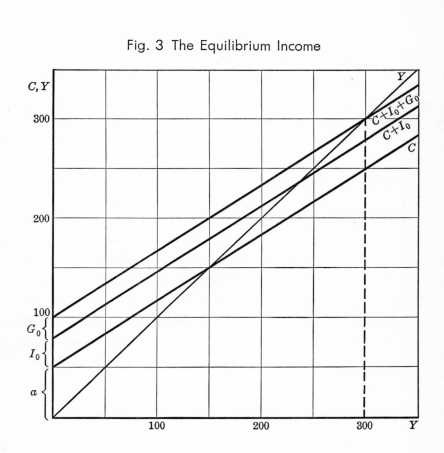

Fig. 3 The Equilibrium Income

rium income is then the point at which this 45-degree line crosses the $C+I_0+G_0$ line—that is, the point at which $Y=C+I_0+G_0$. As in the table, this value is 300 billion dollars.

A study of Table 3 gives us also some understanding of the process by which the economy reaches the equilibrium value. In Chapter 2 we noted that firms were completely neutral in our economy, since all the income received by firms is in turn allocated to consumers. Suppose that consumers expected an income of 240 billion dollars. They would spend 210 billion dollars for consumption. This sum, together with 30 billion dollars of investment and 20 billion dollars of government spending, would mean 260 billion dollars of income to firms and, in turn, to consumers. These consumers would therefore be dissatisfied with their behavior, since their consumption of 210 billion dollars assumed that their income would be only 240 billion dollars, and they would prefer to consume more out of the new, higher income. The increased consumption in turn increases income still further, with the process of expansion continuing until income reaches 300 billion dollars.

The opposite process, contraction, would take place if consumers originally started with the expectation of an income of 360 billion dollars. They would spend 290 billion for consumption, yielding a total income to firms of 340 billion dollars ($290+20+30$ billion). When this income got back to consumers, they would feel that they had overspent their incomes and would contract spending to the lower level appropriate to the lower incomes. This contraction induces further contraction until incomes have fallen to 300 billion dollars and consumption to 250 billion dollars.

A great deal of confusion has revolved around the basic equations and whether or not they are always true. The answer is that equation 1 is always true, for it merely expresses the definition of income as the sum of all expenditures. It therefore must be true, in exactly the same way that the population of New England *must* be the sum of the populations of the six states which are included in the equation cited in Chapter 1. The other equations, 2, 3, and 4, indicate the intended behavior of consumers, investors, and government administrators, respectively. Since they represent behavior, they are true only if we allow sufficient time for the intended behavior to become actual behavior.

As an example, imagine that a small merchant checks his cash-register tape at noon and, on the basis of a half day's business, estimates his total income for the entire day. He calls his wife and tells her that she must do her shopping accordingly. She buys a number of things during the afternoon but passes up a hat she likes because she cannot afford it. That evening, the merchant adds his receipts and finds that his net income was 30 dollars more than he had estimated. He and his wife now see that their actual expenditures were less than they would have been had the estimate been correct. For this household, the consumption function does not hold today. But, if we wait until morning, his wife will buy the hat. At that time, the actual behavior will match their intended behavior.

Other discrepancies might arise if shoppers are unable

to buy the goods for which they are looking. Such difficulties might also face business and government purchasing agents.

Another difference between intended and actual behavior may result from unplanned change in inventories. In Chapter 2, we saw that businesses invest in inventories as well as in plant and equipment. Often such inventories may be part of a regular investment program. However, sometimes businesses buy (or make) goods for further sale and then are unable to find customers. In such cases, the businessman will find himself investing in inventories which he does not want. In the other direction, a firm faced with a sudden rush of business may find that it has depleted its inventories (disinvested) to a greater extent than it wishes.

In all these cases, adjustments can be made if there is enough time. Usually, in fact, the time required for adjustment is quite short. Consumers can alter purchases and firms change their reorder patterns in a moderately short period of time. For this reason, we can ignore the discrepancies between actual and intended behavior if we are thinking of periods of, say, a year, but not if we look at shorter periods. These discrepancies are an important part of the pattern of adjustment toward the equilibrium level.

A complete understanding of our society would require that we direct especial attention to this adjustment process to determine whether it operates correctly and efficiently. Such study constitutes the heart of business-cycle research. Our present aim is to compare various equilibrium levels. We must leave to business-cycle analysis the precise study of how and whether the new equilibrium will be attained.

THE MULTIPLIER

One important application of the analysis given here is in examining changes in aggregate demand in comparison with changes in one of the unexplained variables, especially government expenditures and investment. First, let us examine the effects of a change in investment. We start with equation

(9)
$$Y = \frac{1}{1-b}(a + I_0 + G_0).$$

We shall represent a change in investment by ΔI and the corresponding change in income by ΔY. Then, as investment increases from I_0 to $I_0 + \Delta I$, income will increase from Y to $Y + \Delta Y$. Substituting these values in equation 9, we obtain

(10)
$$Y + \Delta Y = \frac{1}{1-b}(a + I_0 + \Delta I + G_0)$$

$$= \frac{1}{1-b}(a + I_0 + G_0) + \frac{1}{1-b}\Delta I.$$

Subtracting equation 9 from this, we obtain

(11)
$$\Delta Y = \frac{1}{1-b}\Delta I.$$

This equation gives us the ratio between increases in investment and increases in income, which depends upon the marginal propensity to consume, b. On the basis of the figures presented in Tables 2 and 3, in which b equals ⅔, this ratio will be three. The reader can check this by referring to Table 3. If investment increases to 50, the equilibrium income will increase to 360. In this case, the increase of 20 in investment causes an increase of 60 (or three times as much) in income.

This ratio between increases in income and investment is so important that economists have given it the name of the *multiplier*. We shall represent the multiplier by k. We can see from equation 11 that

$$(12) \qquad\qquad k = \frac{1}{1-b}.$$

By a similar set of computations, we find that income will react in the same way to changes in government expenditures—that is,

$$(13) \qquad\qquad \Delta Y = k \Delta G.$$

This should be no surprise, since government expenditures and investment enter the description of our model in exactly the same way. If this explanation is not satisfying, equation 13 can easily be proved by using equations 10 and 11 as models.

The multiplier gives the ratio of changes in equilibrium income to changes in investment. However, to remind ourselves that this is a summary of an economic process, not a juggling of simple algebra, it may be useful to trace the effects of an increase in investment upon income. We shall use a marginal propensity to consume of two-thirds and assume an initial investment of $100. This $100 becomes the income of some consumer, who will spend two-thirds of it, or $66.67. This sum in turn becomes income to someone else, who will spend two-thirds of it, or $44.44. This process continues until the succeeding terms become too small to mention. Each of these can be treated as expenditure or as income. Eventually the total will expand by $300—the initial investment of $100 plus the successive increases in consumption, which total $200. The whole process follows the pattern described in Table 4.

TABLE 4

THE MULTIPLIER

Expenditure	Amount	Income
Initial Investment	$100.00	Income, Consumer A
Consumption, Consumer A	66.67	Income, Consumer B
Consumption, Consumer B	44.44	Income, Consumer C
Consumption, Consumer C	29.63	Income, Consumer D
Consumption, Consumer D	19.75	Income, Consumer E
Consumption, Consumer E	13.17	Income, Consumer F
Consumption, Consumer F	8.78	Income, Consumer G
. . .	. . .	. . .

Total $282.44 (or, eventually, $300.00)

Table 4 indicates that the income in each round serves as the basis of the consumption in the next. In this way, the entire process of expansion takes place as a multiple of the original spending. If consumers anticipate their higher incomes by increasing consumption before the new income is actually received, the entire process could take place almost simultaneously.

If they follow rather conservative spending habits, the expansionary process will take longer, but the end result will be the same.

THE SAVING FUNCTION

Many economists prefer to speak of a saving function rather than of a consumption function. The choice between these terms involves largely a matter of taste rather than a difference in analysis. Since income is either saved or consumed, a decision about consumption is necessarily a decision about saving and *vice versa*. We can obtain the saving function from the consumption function merely by subtracting consumption from income. Using S for saving,

(14)
$$\begin{aligned} S &= Y - C \\ &= Y - (a + bY) \\ &= Y - a - bY \\ &= -a + (Y - bY) \\ &= -a + (1 - b)Y. \end{aligned}$$

The quantity $(1-b)$ is the marginal propensity to save, the amount by which saving increases for every dollar of increased income. The first term, $-a$, gives the level of the saving function. The arithmetical computation of a saving function is presented in Table 5, using the consumption data of Table 2.

As indicated in Table 5, the saving column is obtained by subtracting the consumption at each income level from the income. Thus, for 180 billion dollars, saving is 180 billion

minus 170 billion, or 10 billion dollars. The marginal propensity to save is the ratio of the increased saving to the increased
income for each interval. Since we have assumed straight lines,
the marginal propensity to save is the same at all income levels.

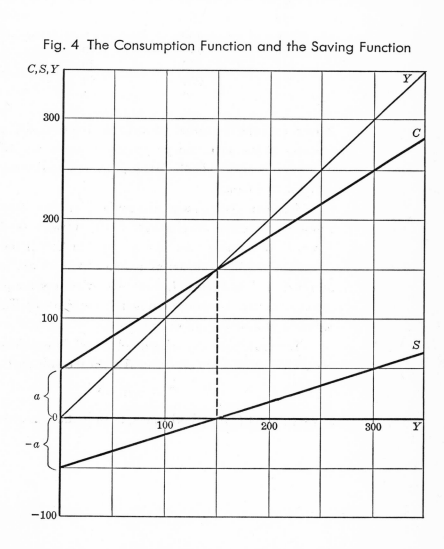

Fig. 4 The Consumption Function and the Saving Function

TABLE 5

HYPOTHETICAL SAVING FUNCTION
(Unit: one billion dollars)

Income	Consumption	Saving	Marginal Propensity to Save
0	50	−50	
			.33
60	90	−30	
			.33
120	130	−10	
			.33
150	150	0	
			.33
180	170	10	
			.33
240	210	30	
			.33
300	250	50	
			.33
360	290	70	

Notice that the marginal propensity to save, .33, is the complement of the marginal propensity to consume, .67; the sum of the two is always 1.00. This indicates that all income is either saved or consumed.

We can also obtain the saving function from the consumption function graphically. First, draw a 45-degree line upward, the income line. The saving function is then obtained by subtracting the consumption function from the income line, as illustrated in Figure 4. Note that when consumption equals income, saving is zero. (Using the numbers of Table 5, this value is at 150 billion dollars.)

The multiplier can also be obtained from this saving relation. The equilibrium is obtained from the rule that

(15) $C + I_0 + G_0 = Y.$

If we subtract C from both sides, the equation can be restated as

(16) $I_0+G_0=Y-C=S.$

Inserting the saving function of equation 14, we obtain

(17) $-a+(1-b)Y=I_0+G_0;$
                       $(1-b)Y=a+I_0+G_0.$

This is the same as equation 9. The rest of the process follows in the same fashion as in equations 10 through 13.

A very simple solution technique corresponds to this. Let us find the equilibrium income from the saving function of Table 5, using again the values of 20 and 30 for I_0 and G_0 respectively.

The equilibrium income is immediately seen to be 300 billion dollars, for only at that level will saving match the sum of I_0 and G_0. Since this sum is 50 billion dollars at all levels of income, we need look only for the income level at which saving also equals 50 billion dollars.

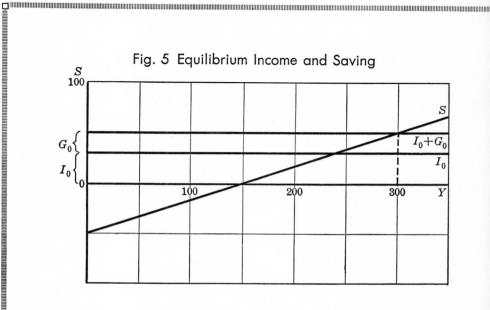

Fig. 5 Equilibrium Income and Saving

TABLE 6

HYPOTHETICAL INCOME DATA
(Unit: one billion dollars)

Y	S	I_0	G_0	$I_0 + G_0$
0	−50	20	30	50
60	−30	20	30	50
120	−10	20	30	50
150	0	20	30	50
180	10	20	30	50
240	30	20	30	50
300	50	20	30	50
360	70	20	30	50

The corresponding graphic solution, demonstrated in Figure 5, is equally simple. If we draw a horizontal line to represent investment plus government spending, the equilibrium income is found at the point at which the saving function crosses this line.

A CONSUMPTION MULTIPLIER?

We have seen that it is possible to construct a multiplier that indicates the relation between changes in investment or government spending and changes in income. Can we then compute a multiplier that will give a relationship between the level of consumption and the level of income?

The answer to this question is no. The purpose of these multipliers is to show the reaction of the basic system to outside forces, the reaction of changes in the *endogenous* variables to changes in the *exogenous* variables. Consumption is not one of these outside forces but is, rather, a built-in feature of the system. To find the level of consumption, we need merely find the level of income, whereas the solution to the corresponding problem for government spending requires a crystal ball.

In a sense, it would be possible to compute something that is partly a consumption multiplier. Equation 2 told us that

(2) $C = a + bY.$

One might think of this equation as dividing consumption into two parts, one that does not depend upon income and one that does. (By analogy with the costs of a firm, we might call these *fixed consumption* and *variable consumption*.) The built-in part is the variable consumption; the fixed consumption might be regarded as exogenous. If so, one might use equation 9—

$$Y = \frac{1}{1-b}(a + I_0 + G_0) -$$

to compute a multiplier:

$$\Delta Y = \frac{1}{1-b}\Delta a.$$

Such a multiplier would be the same as the investment multiplier plus the government-expenditures multiplier. Since a is the constant that indicates the level of the consumption, this multiplier is of limited usefulness in indicating the reaction of national income to shifts in the level of the consumption function. Indeed, it is seldom applied; most economists find it simpler never to use the concept of a consumption multiplier.

POLICY IMPLICATIONS

Even with such a simple model as the one given here, it is possible to discuss a number of important policy questions. If, for example, the society is at a level that is 30 billion dollars below full employment, the multiplier indicates the amount of stimulus that will be required to reach the full-employment level. This stimulus might be either investment or government spending. Similarly, if demand exceeds available production, thus causing inflation, the multiplier indicates the magnitude of the task of reducing aggregate demand. In Chapter 4, we shall discuss especially the effect of the variables that are under control of the government.

PROBLEMS AND DISCUSSION QUESTIONS

1. If $C = 20 + \frac{3}{4}Y$, what is the saving function?
2. If $I = 40$, $G = 30$, and $C = 20 + \frac{3}{4}Y$, what is the equilibrium income?
3. On the basis of the figures above, what is the multiplier?
4. Using the graphs of this chapter as models, draw a graph showing the equilibrium income in the examples above.
5. Explain how the reaction would work through the economy if consumers suddenly decide to consume less (that is, if there is a decrease in a).

SUGGESTED ADDITIONAL READINGS

The material of this chapter consists mainly in a review of elementary income analysis. Additional treatment of this subject can be found in almost any text in principles of economics and especially in Alvin Hansen, *Business Cycles and National Income* (New York: Norton, 1951).

The distinction between definitions and behavioral equations was aptly made by Gottfried Haberler in "Mr. Keynes' Theory of the Multiplier," *Zeitschrift für Nationalökonomie* (1936), reprinted in *Readings in Business Cycle Theory* (Philadelphia: Blakiston, 1944).

CHAPTER 4

Fiscal Policy

THIS CHAPTER concerns itself with the role of the government in determining the over-all level of aggregate demand. We shall limit our discussion to the role of government fiscal policy—*i.e.*, of those activities connected with the income and expenditures of the government. We shall use the following system:

ADDITIONAL VARIABLES:

Endogenous

$$Y_D = \text{Disposable income.}$$

Exogenous

$$Tx = \text{Taxes.}$$
$$Tr = \text{Transfers.}$$

EQUATIONS

(1) $$Y = C + I + G.$$

(2) $C = a + bY_D.$

(3) $I = I_0.$

(4) $G = G_0.$

(5) $Y_D = Y - Tx + Tr.$

(6) $Tx = Tx_0.$

(7) $Tr = Tr_0.$

As the statistics presented in Chapter 2 demonstrate, the various levels of government—local, state, and federal—have played an increasingly important role in the American economy. In recent years, governments have purchased 20 to 25 percent of all goods and services produced in our country. More than half this total has been purchased by the federal government and the remainder by state and local governments. Since such an enormous portion of national purchasing power is concentrated under relatively centralized control, it is not surprising that there should be many suggestions that this power be used to affect the level of demand. The manipulation of government income and expenditures for the maintenance of a suitable level of income is called *fiscal policy.*

There are, of course, many other ways in which the government can affect national income. Every government activity is apt to have some effect upon the level of national income. An anti-trust case which breaks up a monopoly may lead to lower prices and increased output. A new trade treaty could affect the output of our import and export industries and of those industries whose products compete with the imported goods. We confine ourselves to the field of fiscal policy, therefore, merely for the sake of convenience, not because other activities are unimportant. In the long run, the general tenor of the society, as indicated by the other activities of the government, may be far more important than fiscal policy.

Even within this narrow range of fiscal policy, we shall confine ourselves to some rather simple assumptions. We shall speak of changes in taxes without discussing the various kinds of taxes, even though the differences among them are important. For our purposes, a tax is any device for transferring money from the pockets of consumers to the coffers of the government without any direct return to the consumer. (This last qualification is intended to eliminate from the list of taxes government income received from the post office and other such agencies.)

The government budget then consists of three main items: government expenditures, transfers, and taxes. Government expenditures are limited to payments for goods and services. They include such items as salaries of government officials, payments for transportation, and the purchase of millions of items from jet bombers to paper clips. Transfer payments are those payments that are made without any receipt of goods or services by the government, at least in the year in which the payment is made. Transfers include welfare payments, unemployment compensation, pensions to old soldiers, and, with doubtful validity, interest on the government debt. Taxes, as indicated above, are payments *to* the government for which the taxpayer receives no direct return. Taxes are, therefore, exactly the reverse of transfers. The distinguishing element of each is a flow of money unmatched by a corresponding flow of goods. In some cases, we can even match types of transfers with types of taxes to show the similarity of the two elements. A business subsidy (transfer) is just the opposite of a business tax; unemployment compensation is a negative income tax. Thus we should expect, and shall find, that transfers have exactly the same effects as taxes but in the opposite direction.

There is a great temptation among students to insist on relating the sum totals of government receipts and of government expenditures to each other. However, it is not always true that such a relation exists. So long as a government has the power to borrow, there is no reason to assume that its receipts and expenditures will exactly match in any one year. New expenditures may be financed by borrowing, as are many turnpike projects; new taxes may be used to reduce debt; governments may borrow to finance relief payments. Indeed, the federal government, which has the power to create money, could operate an unbalanced budget forever, printing new money to cover the deficit. (The advisability of such a course is debatable and will be discussed later. It is, however, constitutionally possible.)

Since governments have demonstrated their ability to vary one portion of the budget without a corresponding change in other portions, we shall consider changes in government expenditures, transfers, and taxes separately. Thus, when we say that an increase in government expenditures has a certain effect, this is true, *other things being equal*. In particular, we assume no change in taxes. For example, we say that increased taxes are deflationary (*i.e.*, tend to lower national income), but if these higher taxes cause increased government expenditures, the effect of the whole program may be mildly expansionary.

GOVERNMENT EXPENDITURES

In Chapter 3 we found that the government-expenditures multiplier is equal to

(8)
$$k_G = \frac{1}{1-b}.$$

(In Chapter 3, we designated this multiplier as k. In this chapter, we shall be discussing many different multipliers and therefore have designated this one k_G to indicate that it is the multiplier for government expenditures.) This multiplier indicates the change in aggregate demand per dollar of change in government expenditures. The sign of the multiplier is positive, indicating that an increase in government expenditures will increase income and that, conversely, a decrease in government expenditure will decrease income.

TAXES AND TRANSFERS

Before examining the tax and transfer multipliers, let us consider the problem intuitively. A government transfer puts money into the hands of consumers, exactly as would a government expenditure of the same magnitude. The consumers in both cases respend a portion of the money, thereby increasing the incomes of others and increasing their expenditures. Thus, the effects on consumption are the same whether the government hires an accountant or pays a pension to a retired general. The difference between the two cases is that government expenditures bring about increased production of goods and services, whereas the transfers do not. (In the example above, the accountant must work for his money; the general need not.) If a government expenditure of $100 brings about a $300 increase in income, we would expect it to consist of an increase of $100 in government goods or services and $200 in consumer goods. A transfer payment of $100 causes the same $200 increase in consumption but no increase in government goods and services. In this case, the government-expenditures multiplier is three and the transfer multiplier is two.

Regardless of the size of the consumption effect, it is clear that the difference between the expenditures multiplier and the transfer multiplier will result from the inclusion of the original $100 in the pattern for government expenditures, but not in that resulting from the transfer payment. Therefore, the transfer multiplier will always be exactly one less than the government-expenditures multiplier.

The tax multiplier is numerically the same as the transfer multiplier but its opposite in sign. The transfer multiplier is positive, indicating that an increase in transfers will increase national income. We have already noted that taxes are the opposite of transfers: taxes shift money from consumers to the government whereas transfers shift it from the government to consumers. This symmetry indicates that the **tax multiplier** should be the same as the transfer multiplier but negative. The negative multiplier means that an increase in taxes will decrease income, and vice versa.

THE MULTIPLIERS

We now wish to compute the multipliers for each of the three government variables: expenditures, transfers, and taxes. We start with the system of equations given at the beginning of this chapter:

(1) $\qquad\qquad Y = C + I + G.$

(2) $\qquad\qquad C = a + bY_D.$

(3) $\qquad\qquad I = I_0.$

(4) $\qquad\qquad G = G_0.$

(5) $\qquad\qquad Y_D = Y - Tx + Tr.$

(6) $\qquad\qquad Tx = Tx_0.$

(7) $\qquad\qquad Tr = Tr_0.$

Equations 1, 3, and 4 are the same as those used in Chapter 3. However, equation 2 is slightly different. Instead of the relation given in Chapter 3 between consumption and income, we have substituted the rule that consumption is related to *disposable income,* or take-home pay. This substitution is a step in the direction of greater realism, especially in these days of withholding taxes. It suggests that individuals plan their consumption patterns by examining their earned income after taxes plus receipts of pensions and other such unearned income. Equation 5 merely repeats the definition of disposable income given in Chapter 2, and equations 6 and 7 designate taxes and transfers as exogenous—that is, not explainable in terms of such an economic model.

First, we substitute equations 6 and 7 into equation 5, and equation 5 into equation 2, obtaining

$$\textbf{(9)} \qquad \begin{aligned} C &= a + bY_D \\ &= a + b(Y - Tx_0 + Tr_0) \\ &= a + bY - bTx_0 + bTr_0. \end{aligned}$$

We now substitute equations 9, 3, and 4 into equation 1:

$$\textbf{(10)} \qquad \begin{aligned} Y &= C + I + G \\ &= a + bY - bTx_0 + bTr_0 + I_0 + G_0. \end{aligned}$$

Simplifying equation 10, we obtain

$$\textbf{(11)} \qquad Y - bY = a - bTx_0 + bTr_0 + I_0 + G_0;$$

$$\textbf{(12)} \qquad (1-b)Y = a - bTx_0 + bTr_0 + I_0 + G_0;$$

$$\textbf{(13)} \qquad Y = \frac{1}{1-b}(a - bTx_0 + bTr_0 + I_0 + G_0).$$

To obtain the government-expenditures multiplier, increase G_0 to $G_0 + \Delta G$, and Y will increase to $Y + \Delta Y$.

$$\textbf{(14)} \qquad Y + \Delta Y = \frac{1}{1-b}(a - bTx_0 + bTr_0 + I_0 + G_0 + \Delta G)$$

$$= \frac{1}{1-b}(a - bTx_0 + bTr_0 + I_0 + G_0) + \frac{1}{1-b}\Delta G.$$

Subtracting equation 13 from equation 14,

(15) $$\Delta Y = \frac{1}{1-b}\Delta G.$$

To obtain the transfer multiplier, increase Tr_0 to $Tr_0 + \Delta Tr$, with the corresponding shift in Y:

(16)

$$Y + \Delta Y = \frac{1}{1-b}(a - bTx_0 + bTr_0 + b\Delta Tr + I_0 + G_0)$$

$$= \frac{1}{1-b}(a - bTx_0 + bTr + I_0 + G_0) + \frac{1}{1-b}(b\Delta Tr).$$

Subtracting equation 13,

(17) $$\Delta Y = \frac{1}{1-b}(b\Delta Tr) = \frac{b}{1-b}\Delta Tr.$$

In the same way, we could compute the tax relation:

(18) $$\Delta Y = -\frac{b}{1-b}\Delta Tx.$$

From equations 15, 17, and 18, we can find the appropriate multipliers.

(19) Expenditures: $$k_G = \frac{1}{1-b}$$

(20) Transfers: $$k_{Tr} = \frac{b}{1-b}.$$

(21)   Taxes: $k_{Tx} = -\dfrac{b}{1-b}.$

In our verbal discussions of the relative multiplier effects, we saw that the effects of a government transfer would be less than those of an equal government expenditure. Since this difference is exactly the amount of the original expenditure, the transfer multiplier is one less than the expenditures multiplier. This is also shown by the following computation:

$$\textbf{(22)}\quad k_{Tr}+1=\frac{b}{1-b}+1=\frac{b}{1-b}+\frac{1-b}{1-b}=\frac{b+1-b}{1-b}=\frac{1}{1-b}=k_G$$

We can illustrate the effects of such changes by using the data of Chapter 3, in which we found an equilibrium level of income of 300 billion dollars. This example is repeated in Table 7.

TABLE 7

HYPOTHETICAL INCOME DATA
(Unit: one billion dollars)

$Y=Y_D$	C	I_0	G_0	$C+I_0+G_0$
0	50	30	20	100
60	90	30	20	140
120	130	30	20	180
150	150	30	20	200
180	170	30	20	220
240	210	30	20	260
300	250	30	20	300
360	290	30	20	340

This table does not illustrate the effects of changes in taxes or transfers. We may assume that this is the special case in which taxes and transfers cancel each other out so that disposable income and income are identical. Table 7 does show, however, the effects of changes in government expenditures. If G_0 increases to 40, the equilibrium income increases to 360, indicating a multiplier of three (60 divided by 20).

Since taxes and transfers affect national income in the same fashion, although in opposite directions, we shall give an arithmetical example only for taxes. We shall assume that taxes are 20 billion dollars. This illustration is presented in Table 8.

TABLE 8

HYPOTHETICAL INCOME AND TAX DATA
(Unit: one billion dollars)

Y	Tx	Y_D	C	I_0	G_0	$C+I_0+G_0$
20	20	0	50	30	20	100
80	20	60	90	30	20	140
140	20	120	130	30	20	180
200	20	180	170	30	20	220
260	20	240	210	30	20	260
320	20	300	250	30	20	300
380	20	360	290	30	20	340

The consumption function is the same as the one given in Table 7, except that it is here related specifically to disposable income rather than income. The equilibrium condition is still the same, $Y=C+I_0+G_0$. This condition is satisfied at an income of 260 billion dollars—40 billion dollars less than the equilibrium of Table 7. Since this 40-billion-dollar *decrease* in national income is associated with a 20-billion-dollar *increase* in taxes, we find a tax multiplier of minus two. The government-expenditures multiplier is still three, confirming our previous statement that the tax multiplier is negative and is numerically one less than the government-expenditures multiplier.

The graphic solution to this problem is substantially similar to the numerical solution of Table 8. The effect of the tax is recorded by moving the consumption function *horizontally* by the amount of the tax. The reason for this movement is that the tax alters the relation between income and disposable income. An increase in taxes lowers consumption. In the example of Table 8, with a tax of 20 billion dollars, an income of 320 billion dollars represents a disposable income of only 300 billion dollars, and the corresponding consumption. Investment and government spending are added to this new, lower consumption. Except for the shift in the consumption curve, this entire process is analogous to that of Chapter 3.

Figure 6 shows the graphic solution to this problem. The solid lines show the solution without the tax; the dotted lines show the solution with the tax.

TAXES AND SAVING

The effects of either taxes or transfers on saving are very similar to their effects on consumption. First, let us redefine saving:

(23)

$$S = Y_D - C$$
$$= Y - Tx + Tr - C.$$

This is in keeping with the previous discussion in this chapter, which implied that consumption depends upon disposable income, not upon earned income. This will, however, change the equilibrium condition slightly. This condition requires that

(24)

$$Y = C + I + G.$$

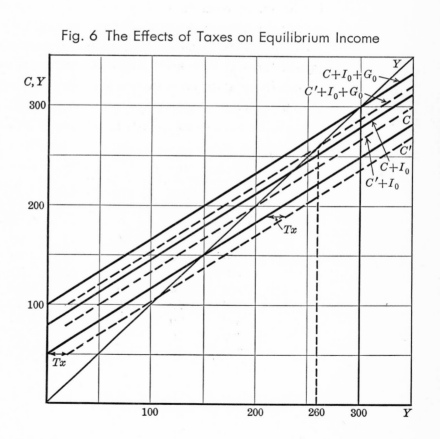

Fig. 6 The Effects of Taxes on Equilibrium Income

Solving equation 23 for Y, we find that

$$\textbf{(25)} \qquad\qquad Y = C + S + Tx - Tr.$$

Substituting this value into equation 24,

$$\textbf{(26)} \qquad\qquad C + S + Tx - Tr = C + I + G,$$

or

$$\textbf{(27)} \qquad\qquad S + Tx - Tr = I + G.$$

This, then, is the new equilibrium condition. In appearance, it seems rather unlike the equilibrium equation presented in Chapter 3. In meaning, however, it is similar. Equation 25 tells us that total receipts $(Y + Tr)$ can be used for consumption, saving, or taxes. Equation 27 says that net outside sources of expenditures $(I + G)$ must equal the net withdrawals of consumers (S) plus the net withdrawals of the government $(Tx - Tr)$ from the income stream.

For the sake of simplicity, let us assume that transfers are

TABLE 9

HYPOTHETICAL INCOME DATA
(Unit: one billion dollars)

$Y = Y_D$	S	I_0	G_0	$I_0 + G_0$
0	−50	20	30	50
60	−30	20	30	50
120	−10	20	30	50
150	0	20	30	50
180	10	20	30	50
240	30	20	30	50
300	50	20	30	50
360	70	20	30	50

TABLE 10

HYPOTHETICAL INCOME AND TAX DATA
(Unit: one billion dollars)

Y	Tx	Y_D	S	$S+Tx$	I_0+G_0
20	20	0	−50	−30	50
80	20	60	−30	−10	50
140	20	120	−10	10	50
170	20	150	0	20	50
200	20	180	10	30	50
260	20	240	30	50	50
320	20	300	50	70	50
380	20	360	70	90	50

zero and consider only taxes. (From an over-all point of view, it is only the difference between taxes and transfers that is effective. If taxes were 30 billion dollars and transfers were 10 billion dollars, we should get the same answers as if taxes were 20 billion dollars and transfers zero.)

The first effect of taxes would be to lower saving at every level, since disposable income decreases as taxes rise. This can be seen by comparison of Table 9, which shows the saving function without taxes, and Table 10, which shows the saving function with a tax of 20 billion dollars. To find the equilibrium income using Table 9, we merely find the point at which saving equals the sum of investment plus government spending. In Table 10, however, it is necessary to add the taxes to the saving and then to find the point at which the sum is equal to investment plus government spending. Since the equilibrium level of income is 300 billion dollars with zero tax and 260 billion dollars with a tax of 20 billion dollars, we find a multiplier of minus two. This is appropriate for a marginal propensity to consume of two thirds.

The same solution is presented in Figure 7. The solid lines represent the saving without the tax. The dotted line, S', indicates the lower saving as the result of the tax. This line represents a horizontal movement of the amount of the tax. The second dotted line $(S' + Tx)$ indicates the addition of the tax to this new saving function. This line represents a vertical movement from S' by the amount of the tax. Thus, the new equilibrium is obtained by a 45-degree shift upward of the saving line.

In Figure 7, and in comparing Tables 9 and 10, we find that at every income level, the new saving plus the tax is higher than the old saving. This is what we would expect, since the tax will fall partly upon consumption. As a result, saving will not decrease as much as the tax rises.

BUILT-IN FLEXIBILITY

A government budget in which taxes, transfers, and, sometimes, government expenditures change with income is said to have "built-in flexibility." The object of such a program is to lessen the influence of changes in investment upon the national income. Rather than examining this program in all its complexity, let us merely compute the multiplier for a system in which taxes change with income, transfers are zero, and government expenditures remain fixed.

In a case of this sort, one would normally expect all reactions in the economy to be more sluggish than otherwise. If the marginal rate of taxation were 25 percent, a decline in earned income of $100 would be a decline in disposable income of only $75. The resulting change in consumption would also be less, as would all successive induced changes in consumption. We would expect the multiplier to be less, as indeed it is.

With h representing the marginal rate of taxation, the system we are discussing consists of:

(28) $$Y = C + I + G;$$

(29) $$C = a + b(Y - Tx);$$

(30) $$Tx = T_0 + hY;$$

(31) $$I = I_0;$$

(32) $$G = G_0.$$

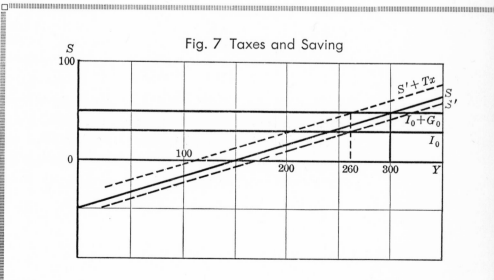

Fig. 7 Taxes and Saving

Substituting equation 30 into equation 29, we have

(33) $$C = a + b(Y - T_0 - hY)$$
$$= a + bY - bT_0 - bhY$$
$$= a - bT_0 + bY - bhY.$$

Substituting equation 31, 32, and 33 into equation 28, we have

(34) $$Y = a - bT_0 + bY - bhY + I_0 + G_0;$$

(35) $$Y - bY + bhY = a - bT_0 + I_0 + G_0;$$

(36) $$Y = \frac{1}{1 - b + bh}(a - bT_0 + I_0 + G_0).$$

Thus, the investment multiplier with built-in flexibility is

(37) $$k_{II} = \frac{1}{1 - b + bh}$$

This multiplier is smaller than the ordinary multiplier, since the extra term increases the denominator of the fraction and thereby lowers the entire fraction. For this reason, the effect of a given change in investment or government spending will be less than if taxes were fixed. This becomes more apparent if we re-examine equation 33:

$$C = a - bT_0 + bY - bhY$$
$$= a - bT_0 + b(1 - h)Y.$$

Since h is the marginal rate of taxation, $(1 - h)$ represents the percentage of additional income that is kept. We might call this a marginal rate of retention. Since b is the marginal propensity to consume retained earnings, $b(1 - h)$ is the effective marginal propensity to consume. Naturally, the higher h is, the lower is the effective propensity. If we compute the multiplier with this effective propensity, it is the same as using a smaller marginal propensity to consume, so of course the multiplier is lower. Table 11 gives the effective rate and the multiplier

TABLE 11

BUILT-IN FLEXIBILITY

b	h	$b(1-h)$	k
.8	.0	.80	5.00
.8	.1	.72	3.57
.8	.2	.64	2.78
.8	.3	.56	2.28
.6	.0	.60	2.50
.6	.1	.54	2.18
.6	.2	.48	1.92
.6	.3	.42	1.72
.4	.0	.40	1.67
.4	.1	.36	1.56
.4	.2	.32	1.47
.4	.3	.28	1.39

for selected values of b and h. The difference in the multipliers for $h=0$ and the other values indicates the effect of built-in flexibility upon the multipliers.

This built-in flexibility has become an important tool of modern fiscal policy. If the government financial program is designed so that taxes fall and transfers rise with every decline in national income, the induced changes in income will be smaller. Such a program helps to keep recessions from becoming depressions. Excise, income, and payroll taxes have this feature, as does unemployment insurance. Property and poll taxes do not have it. Neither do transfer payments, such as pensions, based purely on age or service.

The attractive part of such a program is the built-in feature. Although the multiplier is lessened, it remains greater than one unless the marginal propensity to consume is zero or the marginal rate of taxation is 100 percent. Therefore, it is not possible by such a program to eliminate all fluctuations in income. On the other hand, it is possible to eliminate these fluctuations by a suitable program of change in tax *rates* or government spending. However, these changes require executive planning and, usually, legislative approval, which take time and necessitate correct forecasting techniques. The built-in features, on the other hand, operate automatically, immediately, and without the necessity of prediction.

BALANCED BUDGET

In public discussions about government activity, we sometimes hear the statement that inflation or depression could be avoided if every change in government spending were matched by a corresponding change in taxes. Our previous discussions should convince us that this is not the case, since the multipliers for government expenditures and for taxes are not the same. If the government were to embark upon a program of spending when, and only when, it had tax revenue to cover the spending, then we could say that the government had a marginal propensity to consume of one. Since the marginal propensity of the average taxpayer is less than this, the flow of spending will increase. Thus, increased spending is inflationary even if it is matched by increased taxes. The exact amount of the expansionary effect can be obtained from the multipliers. Let government expenditures and taxes both increase by an amount X—that is,

$$(38) \qquad \Delta G = \Delta Tx = X.$$

Then the increase in income will be the sum of the effects of the increase in both—that is,

$$(39) \qquad \Delta Y = k_G X + k_{Tx} X,$$

letting k_G and k_{Tx} represent the expenditures multiplier and the tax multiplier, respectively. Using the values obtained in earlier equations 19 and 21,

$$(40) \qquad \begin{aligned} \Delta Y &= \frac{1}{1-b} X - \frac{b}{1-b} X \\ &= \frac{1-b}{1-b} X \\ &= X \end{aligned}$$

From the foregoing, we may conclude that the balanced-budget multiplier is exactly one, regardless of the marginal propensity to consume. We can see this by imagining the following case. Suppose the government imposes a special tax on accountants and uses the money so acquired to hire the same accountants to audit government books. The accountants end up with the same amount of money, so their consumption is unaffected. The net increase in national product will be the extra work these accountants did for the government. If we assume that the government gets its money's worth, the net effect of the increased tax and expenditure will be to increase the national income by exactly the same amount.

A FINAL CAUTION

The preceding discussion has centered around the effects of changes in government fiscal variables, assuming that other factors do not change. As we shall see in Chapter 9 it is very unlikely that investment would be unaffected by changes in government fiscal variables. In the interests of simplicity, however, in our discussion of the effect of the fiscal changes we shall assume that investment is unchanged. Then we shall consider the effects of any resultant change in investment as an added factor, after the groundwork has been prepared (see Chap. 16).

Within this limited framework, our conclusions are limited still more, to the mechanics of government fiscal policy. The only conclusions to be drawn deal with what the government *can* do, not with what it *should* do. The government *can* provide any desired level of aggregate demand; many citizens feel it *should* not do so, because, they claim, such expansion leads us down the road to socialism or serfdom, or because it would be better to encourage private initiative, or because such government activities lead to certain undesirable results that may be worse than a mild recession. But the question of the merits of such a course cannot be answered here. Some of its aspects require additional analysis, and we shall discuss them in more detail later. Many of them depend upon value judgments, and the most that an economist can do is to point out what the alternatives are.

This distinction between *can* and *should* is the source of most of the confusion over the term *Keynesian*. To the extent that he follows the analysis above of what *can* be done, virtually every economist is a Keynesian. To the extent that they believe that the government *should* affect national income in one or more ways, at one particular time or always, different people are Keynesian to different degrees. In the sense of advocating high government expenditures at all times, it is doubtful if there has ever been a Keynesian, even Lord Keynes. Economists are in substantial agreement in the analytical areas. In policy recommendations, they agree on what ought to be done about as often and as rarely as other citizens.

PROBLEMS AND DISCUSSION QUESTIONS

In the first four problems below, assume that $C = 20 + \frac{3}{4} Y_D$, $I = 40$, and $G = 30$.

1. If taxes are 10 and transfers zero, what is the equilibrium level of national income?

2. If the government wishes to push national income to 360, by how much must it alter government spending? transfer payments? taxes?

3. If the government increases spending by 20 billion dollars and

finances half the increase by taxation, how much will national income change?

4. If taxes equal $-10 +.10\dot{Y}$, what is the investment multiplier?

5. What kinds of transfer payments are part of a program of built-in flexibility?

6. Is the built-in flexibility of our tax system altered by changes in family exemptions for income taxes? by changes in income-tax rates?

SUGGESTED ADDITIONAL READINGS

The balanced-budget multiplier was first pointed out in Trygve Haavelmo, "Multiplier Effects of a Balanced Budget," *Econometrica*, XIII (October 1945). See also the subsequent discussion in the same journal in April 1946.

Among the leading advocates of built-in flexibility is the Committee for Economic Development, a business group concerned with economic and fiscal policy. For comments on its proposals see O. H. Brownlee, "The C. E. D. on Federal Tax Reform," *Journal of Political Economy*, LVI (1948), and R. A. Musgrave and M. H. Miller, "Built-in Flexibility," *American Economic Review*, XXXVIII (1948).

On general fiscal policy, see Alvin H. Hansen, *Business Cycles and National Income* (New York: Norton, 1951).

CHAPTER 5

The Marginal Efficiency of Capital

C HAPTER 9 contains an extended discussion of the determinants of investment. At this stage, however, we must
pause to consider the mechanics of investment calculation. Naturally, this discussion will not give detailed attention
to all the factors that affect investment, but it will indicate the
kinds of problems that face the investor. Throughout this discussion, it is well to remember that investment for the whole
society consists only in new physical goods to be used in further
production. If one individual buys securities from another
individual, his investment is counteracted by the other man's
sale. If the individual purchases newly issued stock, he merely
transfers his money to a corporation, receiving from the corporation a claim against its future income. Only when the corporation uses this money to buy buildings, machinery, or inventories
has any real investment taken place. We are therefore discussing
the problems of the corporate manager, not of the stockholder.

In a simple sense, the problem of investment is trivial: a

businessman will make any investment if he and his backers think it will be profitable. To examine the problems of determining profitability, let us consider the problem of a firm trying to decide whether to purchase a specific asset—say, a truck to be used for commercial hauling. The firm can expect, for each year it owns the truck, to receive certain fees for hauling. We may refer to these fees, over the years, as a *stream of revenues*. The firm must also expect to incur each year a number of out-of-pocket costs, for taxes, gasoline, oil, tires, wages of truck drivers, and all the other expenses of doing business. Let us call these a *stream of costs*. The difference between these streams of revenues and costs constitutes a *stream of net returns* for the truck.

Against these net returns, spread through future years, the firm must match the original cost of the truck. It is obvious that these net returns must cover the depreciation on the truck. A moment's reflection, however, indicates that the stream of net revenues must also cover the cost of financing the original purchase. If a firm borrows money for such a purchase, it must pay interest; if it uses its own money, it must forego alternative opportunities. For the sake of simplicity, let us assume that the firm borrows the money. It is then meaningful to ask: "At what interest rate could it borrow money to buy the truck and still break even?" In more formal terms, this question becomes "What interest rate makes the present value of the returns (or the *yield*) equal to the purchase price?" The firm would buy the truck only if the prospective yield is greater than the interest rate at which it borrows.

The yield on investments is called the *marginal efficiency of capital.* It is called *efficiency* because it indicates a *rate* of net return over cost; it is called *marginal* because it refers only to additions to total capital, not to the yield of existing capital assets. (Even though the return on an existing railroad may be 30 percent, the return on a second railroad planned to serve the same towns might be very low, or even negative.)

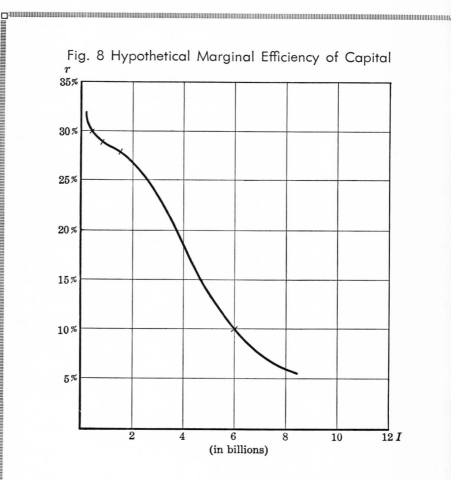

Fig. 8 Hypothetical Marginal Efficiency of Capital

If we imagine similar computations for every business-man who contemplates making an investment, we can conceive a marginal-efficiency-of-capital schedule for the society. Thus, there could be, at a given time, 500-million-dollars' worth of projects yielding 30 percent or more, 400-million-dollars' worth yielding 29 percent, and 600-million-dollars' worth yielding 28 percent. Adding as we go, we could compute the number of projects yielding as much as, or more than, a given return. In our example above, there are 900 million dollars yielding 29 percent or more, 1,500 million yielding 28 percent, and so on. Such a tabulation is shown in Figure 8.

We would expect businessmen to make investments that yield more than the market rate of interest. Therefore, if we knew the marginal-efficiency-of-capital schedule and the market rate of interest, we could find the amount of investment that would take place. From Figure 8, we learn that at 10 percent there would be six billion dollars of new investment. Given the marginal-efficiency-of-capital schedule, we could find the amount of investment if we knew the rate of interest. We say, then, that investment is a *function* of the rate of interest. (Remember the definition of function given in Chapter 1.) If we knew the form of this function, even approximately, we could state it alge-braically and include it in our system as we did the consump-tion function. Unfortunately, we do not have such information and must content ourselves with the general idea of a function. We write

(1) $$I = f(r)$$

to indicate that investment is a function of the rate of interest. (Read this equation as "I equals f of r," not "f times r.")

The principles of investment given here do not change if we relax our assumption that all investments are made with borrowed money. We should not expect businessmen to invest their own funds in projects that yield less than the market rate of interest, for they have other, more profitable uses for their money. The factors that affect investment are summarized in Figure 9.

The principal objection to the marginal-efficiency-of-capital concept is that it conceals more than it explains. To explain changes in the marginal efficiency of capital, we would have to explain changes in the purchase price of capital goods and in the expected net return. The latter depends upon expected costs and expected revenues. Although we have assumed that these are given, the most interesting problems of business forecasting

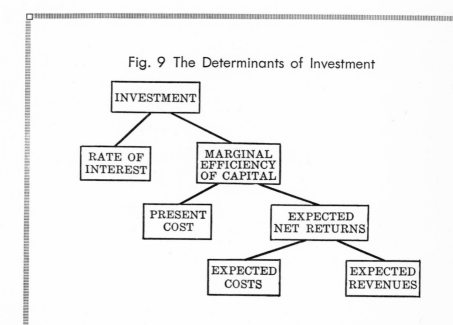

Fig. 9 The Determinants of Investment

and business psychology center around these expectations. There is full range for elaborate statistical techniques, for political opinions, and for the businessman's own natural optimism or pessimism. Because of their subjective nature, these factors cannot be analyzed completely, but we shall postpone even an incomplete discussion to Chapter 9. Meanwhile, we shall use the marginal-efficiency-of-capital concept, bearing in mind that it is correct but incomplete.

NUMERICAL COMPUTATIONS

There remains one final problem: the numerical computation of the marginal efficiency of capital. Such calculations are treated fully in texts on the mathematics of investment, but we may summarize them here.

First, let us imagine a machine that costs $1,000, lasts for only one year, and whose product can be sold at the end of the year for $1,080 above out-of-pocket costs. For such a machine, the marginal efficiency of capital is 8 percent, for at that rate it would be possible to borrow the $1,000, repay the principal ($1,000) and the interest ($80) at the end of the year, and just break even. Such an investment would be profitable at any rate below 8 percent, unprofitable above it. If we call the present value Q and the return R,

(2) $$Q(1+r) = R:$$

(3) $$\$1,000 \ (1.08) = \$1,080.$$

Note that it was necessary to multiply by $(1+r)$, since the borrower must repay the principal *and* the interest.

Similarly, we could find the present value, knowing the return, by

(4) $$Q = \frac{R}{(1+r)}.$$

(5) $$\$1,000 = \frac{\$1080}{1.08}.$$

In a simple case like this, it would be possible to solve directly for *r*. However, we might also do so by a simple process of trial and error. At 6 per cent, the present value of $1,080 in one year is $1,019 $\left(\dfrac{\$1,080}{1.06}\right)$; at 8 percent, $1,000 $\left(\dfrac{\$1,080}{1.08}\right)$; and at 10 percent, $982 $\left(\dfrac{\$1,080}{1.10}\right)$. Since the cost is $1,000, the marginal efficiency of capital is 8 percent, for at that rate the present value equals the cost.

If this machine were to yield its $1,080 only at the end of the second year, the marginal efficiency would be slightly less than 4 percent. If we borrowed money at 4 percent to buy the machine, we would owe $1,040 $(1.04 \times \$1,000)$ at the end of the first year and $1,081.60 $(1.04 \times \$1,040)$ at the end of the second year. Actually, the marginal efficiency would be 3.92 percent. The formula for such a computation would be

(6) $$(1+r)^2 Q = R:$$

(7) $(1.0392)^2 \times \$1000 = \$1080,$

or it could be stated as

(8) $Q = \dfrac{R}{(1+r)^2}.$

If the return came at the end of three years, the divisor would be $(1+r)^3$; at the end of four years, $(1+r)^4$; and so on.

Most investments, in fact, do not yield a single return but, rather, a return for each of many years, or even for each month or day. In such cases, the present value of the stream is the sum of the present values of each return in the stream. If R_1, R_2, . . . R_n are the returns in each year; Q_1, Q_2 . . . , Q_n the present values of each of these returns; and Q the overall present value, then

(9) $Q = Q_1 + Q_2 + \ldots + Q_n$

$$= \frac{R_1}{1+r} + \frac{R_2}{(1+r)^2} + \ldots + \frac{R_n}{(1+r)^n}.$$

The marginal efficiency of capital is that value of r that makes the present value equal to the original purchase price. To find this value, insert the values of the returns $(R_1, R_2, \ldots R_n)$, set Q equal to the purchase price, and solve for r. If the machine will last for more than two years, this solution is extremely difficult. It is usually easier to guess at a value for r, solve for Q, and compare the result with the cost. If Q is greater than the cost, the guess was too high. We can then keep trying until we find the marginal efficiency of capital.

PROBLEMS AND DISCUSSION QUESTIONS

The following problems are intended to clarify the arithmetical process of determining the marginal efficiency of capital.

1. Company A is considering the purchase of a machine which costs 1,000 dollars, will last for two years, and is expected to produce 500 units of output per year. These products sell at $4.00 and use raw materials costing $1.50 each. The machines will require 250 labor hours per year at $1.70 per hour. Selling cost for this product is estimated at $22 per month.

    a. Find the net annual return for this machine. Do not deduct depreciation.

    b. Assuming that all costs and revenues are concentrated at the end of each year, find the present value of the return if the interest rate is 6 percent.

    c. Find the present value at 8 percent.

    d. Find the present value at 10 percent.

    e. What is the marginal efficiency of capital for this machine?

2. Other companies are considering the purchase of machines with the following costs and marginal efficiencies:

Company	Cost	Marginal efficiency
B	$10,000	7%
C	7,000	12
D	30,000	5
E	5,000	15
F	22,000	10

Draw up the marginal-efficiency-of-capital schedule for these six companies (including A).

3. What amount of investment will take place if the market rate of interest is 9 percent? if the interest rate is 6 percent?

SUGGESTED ADDITIONAL READINGS

The simple analysis of investment decision discussed here is amplified in J. M. Keynes, *The General Theory of Employment, Interest and Money* (New York: Harcourt Brace, 1936), Chapter 11. This chapter also discusses some of the previous history of the concept. For more advanced discussion, see Chapter 9 of the present volume and the bibliography thereto.

CHAPTER 6

The Commodity Market

N CHAPTER 3 we discussed the determination of the level of income. We saw that there is a specific income corresponding to each level of investment, and that changes in income are related by the multiplier to changes in investment. In Chapter 5 we discussed the marginal-efficiency-of-capital schedule, which relates investment to the rate of interest. By applying the multiplier to this schedule, we can derive the income response to every change in the rate of interest. We shall not compute an interest multiplier, for this would require knowledge of the exact shape of the marginal-efficiency schedule. Rather, we shall summarize the relations that we have previously discussed into a single relationship, giving income as a function of the rate of interest.

It is necessary to investigate the money market to see what factors determine the rate of interest. At the moment, we shall content ourselves with explaining a *schedule*, relating income and the rate of interest. (What we are doing is analogous to deriving a supply curve or a demand curve. Our work here will not enable us to determine either the rate of interest or the level of income, just as a demand curve alone will not tell us the price or the quantity.) Our schedule will be derived from the following system:

VARIABLES:

Endogenous:

Y = Income.

C = Consumption.

I = Investment.

S = Saving.

Exogenous:

G = Government expenditures.

r = Rate of interest.

EQUATIONS:

(1) $Y = C + I + G$.

(2) $C = a + bY$.   (Consumption function)

(3) $I = f(r)$.   (Marginal efficiency of capital)

(4) $S = Y - C$.

(5) $G = G_0$.

In order to find the relationship between income and the rate of interest, we start with a rate of interest chosen at random. From equation 3, the marginal efficiency of capital, we can find the level of investment that corresponds to this rate. If we take this level of investment, the level of government expenditure

(G_0), and the consumption function, the analysis presented in Chapter 3 will enable us to find the level of income corresponding to the rate of interest with which we started. By repeating this process for another rate of interest, we can find a second level of income. Repeating the process for a sufficient number of rates of interest will give us a complete function.

Each of the points on this schedule represents a combination of the rate of interest and the level of income that would result from the adjustment of consumers and investors, given the behavior of the government. Since this adjustment consists of variation in the purchase of goods and services, we may refer to such actions as taking place in the commodity market. For each rate of interest, there is one level of income that represents *equilibrium*—that is, a level from which there is no tendency to depart, either through the actions of consumers or through the actions of investors. Because each point represents such an equilibrium as far as purchases of goods and services are concerned, we refer to such a function as the *commodity equilibrium curve*.

In principle, the method given above for deriving this schedule is quite correct. In practice, it is usually somewhat easier to use the saving function than the consumption function.

From equations 2 and 4 we obtain:

(6)
$$S = Y - C$$
$$= Y - (a + bY)$$
$$= Y - a - bY$$
$$= -a + (1 - b)Y.$$

This last relationship is called the saving function, as it was in Chapter 3. There we also found that the equilibrium condition is

$$
\begin{aligned}
S &= Y - C \\
&= (C + I + G) - C \\
&= I + G.
\end{aligned}
$$

(7)

Now let us repeat the process of deriving the commodity equilibrium curve, using the marginal-efficiency-of-capital schedule (equation 3), the equilibrium condition (equation 7), and the saving function (equation 6). We choose a rate of interest at random. From the marginal efficiency of capital (equation 3), we find the resulting level of investment. Adding this level of investment to the level of government spending, we find the required amount of saving (equation 7). From the saving function (equation 6), we find the level of income that will produce this level of saving. Repeating this process for other rates of interest, we derive other levels of income. By plotting each of these combinations, we produce a commodity equilibrium curve.

This process can be used in a numerical fashion. The subparts of Table 12 give the schedules which correspond to each of the equations given.

Let us assume a rate of interest of 20 percent. From the marginal efficiency of capital (Part A), we find that the resulting rate of investment will be five billion dollars. Using this rate of investment and assuming government expenditures of 25 billion dollars, we find, from Part B, an equilibrium level of saving of 30 billion dollars. From the saving function (Part C), we find that this will result from a level of income of 240 billion

TABLE 12

DERIVATION OF A HYPOTHETICAL COMMODITY EQUILIBRIUM CURVE
(Unit: one billion dollars)

Part A: Marginal Efficiency of Capital		Part B: Equilibrium Level of Saving*		Part C: Saving Function†	
r	I	I	S	Y	S
20%	5	5	30	0	−50
15	15	10	35	60	−30
10	25	15	40	120	−10
5	35	20	45	150	0
		25	50	180	10
		30	55	210	20
		35	60	240	30
		40	65	270	40
				300	50
				330	60
				360	70

* Assuming government expenditures of 25 billion dollars.
† This is the function of Table 5, with additional intermediate values given.

dollars. This gives us one point on the commodity equilibrium curve. Similarly, we find an income of 270 billion dollars corresponding to 15 percent, and an income of 330 billion dollars corresponding to 5 percent. We list these values in Table 13. The student should fill in the income corresponding to the rate of 10 percent.

The same process can be performed graphically. Figure 10 corresponds exactly to Table 12. The process also corresponds.

Part A. Choose a rate of interest at random—say, 20 percent. From the marginal-efficiency-of-capital schedule we find

TABLE 13

HYPOTHETICAL COMMODITY EQUILIBRIUM CURVE
(Unit: one billion dollars)

r	Y
20%	240
15	270
10	
5	330

the corresponding level of investment, five billion dollars. Part
A is merely Figure 8 (p. 75).

Part B. To find the equilibrium level of saving, we must
now add to the five billion dollars of investment the 25 billion
of government expenditure. To do this, we draw a 45-degree
line upward starting from 25 billion dollars, the assumed G_0.
Thus, when I equals 0, S equals 25; and for every dollar of increase in investment, saving also increases by one dollar. In
our particular case, we find saving of 30 billion dollars corresponding to investment of five billion.

Part C. From the saving function, we find the level of income (240 billion dollars) that corresponds to the saving level
of 30 billion dollars. Part C is the same as Figure 5 (p. 43).

Part D. Plot this income (240 billion dollars) against the
20-percent rate of interest with which we started.

Repeating the process for other rates of interest gives other
income values. When these are all plotted in Part D, they can be
connected to produce the commodity equilibrium curve. Part D
corresponds to Table 13.

The parts of Figure 10 have been drawn so that the scales

run exactly the same. In this way, a line drawn parallel to one of the axes will cut two graphs at the same value. The line drawn upward from five billion dollars' investment in Part *A* hits Part *B* at five billion dollars' investment; the line drawn across from Part *B* at 30 billion dollars' saving hits Part *C* at 30 billion dollars' saving. The construction of Part *D* then consists of finding the fourth corner of the rectangle whose base is drawn at 20-percent interest and whose corners are the graphs of Parts *A*, *B*, and *C*. A new rectangle is drawn at 5 percent,

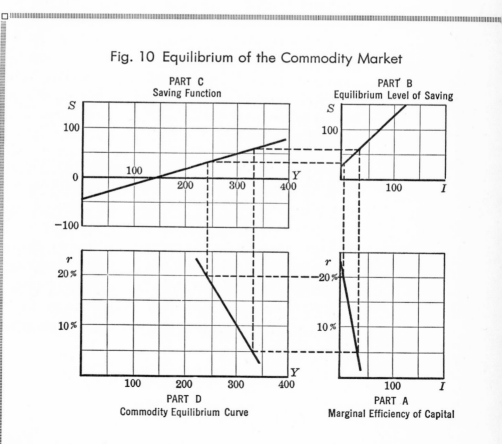

Fig. 10 Equilibrium of the Commodity Market

and finally enough points are available to construct the graph of Part *D*.

This commodity equilibrium curve which we have derived is merely a summary of the functions with which we started. Therefore, any change in any of the basic functions will cause a change in the commodity equilibrium curve. The student should prove for himself that an increase in government expenditures, an increase in the marginal efficiency of capital, or a decrease in the saving function will move the commodity equilibrium curve to the right; opposite shifts will move it to the left. The multipliers presented in Chapter 4 give the ratio between changes in government expenditure and the horizontal movement of the commodity equilibrium curve. The investment multiplier gives the ratio between a horizontal shift of the marginal efficiency of capital and the horizontal shift of the commodity equilibrium curve.

We are not prepared to say anything about the equilibrium level of income until we know something about the rate of interest. To understand the level of the rate of interest, it is necessary to examine the structure of the money market. Some people will feel that such study is unnecessary since the government is a very important part of the money market. Such people summarize the money market thus: The government chooses a rate of interest, then does whatever is necessary to produce that rate of interest. If we believed this to be true, we could add an additional equation:

(8) $$r = r_0,$$

indicating that the rate of interest is an exogenous variable determined by the government for its own reasons. We would then say that economics can be divided into two parts: real economics, dealing with goods and services produced at a fixed interest rate; and monetary theory, which teaches Treasury officials how to fix the interest rate. This view might be partly justified, but it is better for us to examine the money market and see for ourselves what is involved in "pegging" the interest rate. Only in this way can we understand the relations between fiscal policy and monetary policy. Those who prefer to omit such study may insert equation 8, representing it by a horizontal line on Part D of Figure 10. For those who prefer some such understanding, Chapter 7 reviews briefly the workings of the money market.

PROBLEMS AND DISCUSSION QUESTIONS

1. $C = 20 + \frac{3}{4}Y$ and $G = 30$. The marginal efficiency-of-capital schedule is as follows:

r	I
20%	20
15	30
10	40
5	50

Draw up the commodity equilibrium curve.

2. For the information presented in problem 1, show the graphic derivation of the commodity equilibrium curve. (Use Figure 10 as a model.)

3. What would be the commodity equilibrium curve if G were 20 instead of 30 in problem 1?

SUGGESTED ADDITIONAL READINGS

The basic concepts of the commodity market and money market are described by J. R. Hicks in "Mr. Keynes and the Classics," *Econometrica* (April 1937), reprinted in *Readings in the Theory of Income Distribution* (Philadelphia: Blakiston, 1946). The commodity equilibrium curve discussed here corresponds to Hicks's $S=I$ curve; the money equilibrium curve of Chapter 7 corresponds to his $M_D=M_S$ curve.

The Money Market

INTEREST is the price paid by the borrower to the lender of money. Therefore, our discussions of the money market are also discussions of the rate of interest, for anything that affects borrowing and lending will affect the interest rate. Interest has already come to our attention in preceding chapters because it has an important effect upon the level of investment. Now we must consider the factors that determine the rate of interest.

In this chapter, we shall assume, for purposes of the discussion, that there is such a thing as *the* rate of interest. As a matter of fact, there is a range of rates of interest and an even wider variation in *apparent* rates of interest. Government bonds carry interest rates as low as $\frac{3}{4}$ of 1 percent and as high as $3\frac{1}{2}$ percent. State and municipal bonds carry somewhat higher interest rates, corporation bonds higher still. If you wish to borrow money to buy a house, the interest rate is $4\frac{1}{2}$ to 6 percent; to buy a new automobile, 8 to 12 percent; and a personal loan from a small-loan company carries a charge of 3 percent per month—a total of 36 percent per year.

What causes these variations? In large part, they are the result of other costs which are often stated as part of the rate of interest but which are actually payments for something other than the mere lending of money. Foremost among these other costs is the risk premium. A man might be willing to give up the use of his money for a year for 6 percent if he is certain to get the money back. However, if there is a chance that the money may not be returned, he will demand a higher payment to compensate him for his risk. If the lender has found that for every 20 borrowers who repay there is one who does not, he will charge each of the 20 an extra 5 percent to recover the loss incurred on the loan which is *not* repaid. Naturally, the less risky the loans, the lower will be the premium. This is why the federal government can borrow money at a very low rate of interest, for the risk premium is negligible. This risk premium also accounts for many of the variations in rates paid by states and municipalities.

Many loans involve large amounts of clerical expense. For this reason, any small loan will carry a very high "interest rate" merely to cover the administrative costs. At the small-loan rate—36 percent per year—the charge on a one-month loan of $25 would be $.75. Even at this rate, the company probably loses money on such a loan, for the 75-cent charge must cover the cost of checking credit references, recording the loan, and accepting and recording the repayment. Any firm which makes a loan as small as $25 therefore usually does so only for advertising purposes.

After all these other charges are subtracted from the apparent interest rate, there still remain substantial variations in the "pure" rate of interest. Such variations usually depend upon the period of the loan and are related to opportunities which may be foregone by holding the loan. A person who lends money for three months knows that he will have the principal and interest back at the end of that period of time. If new opportunities should develop within that period, he will soon have funds to take advantage of them. Since such a loan is almost the same as cash, it carries an interest rate almost the same as cash —that is, near zero. (In the United States during World War II, one could earn less than two dollars by lending a thousand dollars to the government for three months.) The longer the loan commitment, the greater the chance of passing up a good opportunity. If you lend money for 20 years at, say, 4 percent, it is quite possible that at some time during the 20 years you will have an opportunity to invest the money at 6 percent. For this reason, lenders demand, and receive, higher payments on long-term securities to compensate for the possible alternatives that have been foregone. Thus, even the "pure" rate of interest may vary from, say, 1 to $3\frac{1}{2}$ percent, depending upon the duration of the loan.

Our primary concern with the rate of interest is its effect on investment. Since investments are usually made for relatively long periods, we are most interested in the long-term rate of interest, and we shall speak as though it were the only one. It probably makes little difference which rate we discuss, for long- and short-term rates tend to fluctuate at the same time and to about the same degree. Any movement in the long-term rate is usually matched by a corresponding movement in shorter-term rates. Because the rates are so interrelated, the factors that explain one (the long-term rate) explain all of them.

TRANSACTIONS DEMAND FOR MONEY

Since the interest rate is the price of money, we must consider now the supply of and demand for money. The term *supply of and demand for money* is apt to be confusing, so it will pay us to pause a moment for definitions. What we mean by *money* is a certain *stock* of funds rather than a *flow* of spending power. In common usage, we speak of a desire for money to pay our current bills, for the landlord, the grocer, the gas station. This is a desire for income. One might imagine paying all these bills without ever having any stock of money. If all purchases were made on credit and paid for by check simultaneously with depositing a pay check, all the things for which we say we want money would be supplied without our having any money balance more than temporarily. By a demand for money, we are referring to a desire to have an average balance in the checking account of, say, $500, or to be able to carry $50 in our pocket. In accordance with common usage, we will define money to include currency, coins, and bank deposits.

Elementary textbooks point out that money is a medium of exchange and a store of value. These two uses constitute the demand for money. For the sake of simplicity, we shall assume temporarily that the two uses are independent so that we can discuss them separately.

As a medium of exchange, money is needed to finance transactions. If, as we imagined above, we made all purchases on credit and paid for them by check, no money would be needed. If the whole society operated in the same way, all transactions could be financed by an elaborate juggling of credits the first of every month. Because our entire society does not operate in this fashion, some average stock of money is needed to finance the time intervals between receipt of income and its expenditure on consumption. Similarly, firms need some stock of money to pay bills for goods which are purchased and later sold. The more transactions there are in a society, the greater the stock of money required for these time intervals. The greater the use of credit, the less money is required. If consumption spending were distributed uniformly and if income were received once a month, the stock of money required by a consumer would range from 30 days' consumption (at the beginning of the month) down to zero (at the end), averaging a half month's expenses. If many items are paid for at the beginning of the month, the required stock for the remainder of the period will be less. If all business were in the control of a single large corporation, little money would be needed for interfirm transactions; if all firms were very small, much would be needed.

If we knew the total number of transactions in the society, it would be fairly easy to obtain a simple measure of the amount of money required to finance them. Although some work has been done on this subject, our measures are still rather crude. It seems probable, though, that in a given state of economic organization, the larger the national income, the more transactions there will be, and the more money will be required to finance them. For this reason, we can state the transactions demand for money as a function of income. If we represent the transactions demand as M_1, we can state this demand as

(1) $$M_1 = T(Y).$$

Here again we have a general function, to be read "M_1 equals T of Y." This statement indicates that if we knew the level of income, we could find the amount of M_1. We have not enough information about this function to give its precise characteristics, other than the fact that it should slope upward (the higher the income, the more money required for transactions). Figure 11 gives a reasonable shape for this function.

Equation 1 represents the transactions demand for money as M_1. Since this demand is for currency and bank balances for day-to-day use, it is sometimes referred to as a demand for *active* balances.

LIQUIDITY PREFERENCE

The second aspect of the demand for money is as a store of value, a demand for more passive balances. At first thought, it might seem strange that anyone would wish to use money for this purpose when he could hold assets that earn an income. But when a person buys assets, such as bonds or other securities, he gives up control of his money for a time. In so doing, he renders himself unable to take advantage of future opportunities and becomes more vulnerable to future adversity. He can, of course, sell these assets in an attempt to regain his money, but he cannot always sell them at par value. If the current interest rate is 5 percent, no one would be willing to buy a 4-percent bond at par. The longer the period of time the old bond has left to run at the lower rate, the greater the discount if it is sold. The potential capital loss is a deterrent to any purchaser of securities. Any investor who expects the interest rate to rise will hold cash rather than risk paying a premium to recover control of his funds.

The strength of this preference for liquidity varies from time to time, especially as interest rates change. When rates are low, one would expect that any changes will be upward. Thus, an investor would be foolish to risk a capital loss for a relatively small current return. At such a time, many investors will prefer cash and few will prefer securities. When interest rates are high, the opposite is true. One would expect only downward

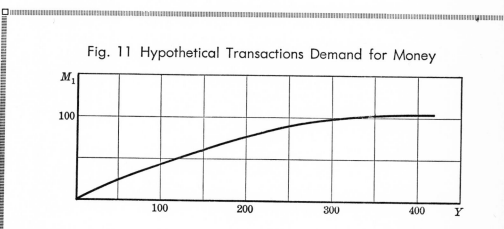

Fig. 11 Hypothetical Transactions Demand for Money

movements of rates, causing capital gains. Since current returns are also high in this case, most investors will forego liquidity and exchange cash for securities. Therefore, the demand for money as a store of value varies inversely with the rate of interest: the higher the rate of interest, the lower the demand for money; the lower the rate of interest, the higher the demand for money. Since this second demand for money depends upon the desire for liquidity, it is called the *liquidity-preference function* and is stated as in equation 2:

(2) $M_2 = L(r).$

Again we have presented merely a general function, without specification as to its shape. However, we have already given

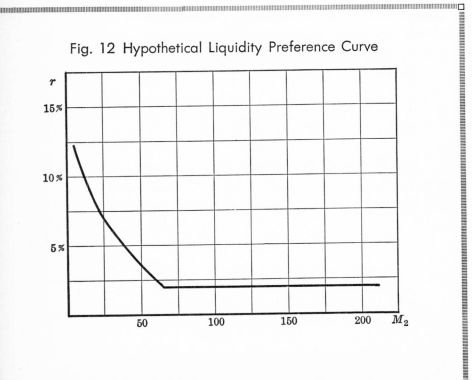

Fig. 12 Hypothetical Liquidity Preference Curve

reasons for believing that it will slope downward. The same kind of reasoning leads us to believe that at a low rate of interest, security buyers would hold any amount of cash rather than bid for securities. At this interest rate, the demand for money becomes perfectly elastic, since the risk of capital loss from an increase in the interest rate is high, and the return is negligible. We therefore expect the liquidity-preference curve to look rather like Figure 12.

Although Figure 12 is intended only to indicate the general shape of the function, statistical observations lend credence to this curve. Figure 13, which illustrates the results of one such statistical experiment, shows a scatter of points not unlike those in Figure 12.

In our further study, we will assume that the interest rate

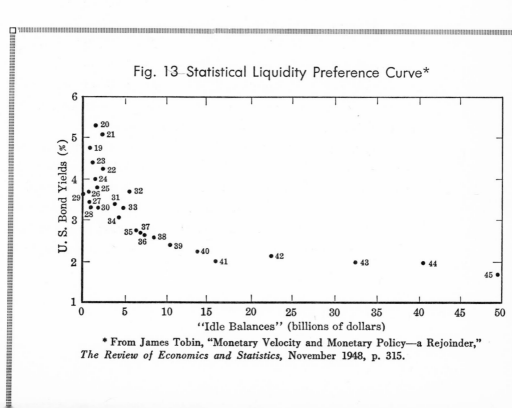

Fig. 13 Statistical Liquidity Preference Curve*

* From James Tobin, "Monetary Velocity and Monetary Policy—a Rejoinder," *The Review of Economics and Statistics*, November 1948, p. 315.

is affected by the amount of M_2 that is available. By what process does this interest-rate adjustment come about? Let us assume that there is a sudden increase in the money supply over and above that needed for ordinary transactions. If investors were previously satisfied with the proportion of cash to securities, they will not wish to hold this additional sum of cash and will try to buy securities. The increased demand for securities will tend to drive up the price of securities, since the present holders will also prefer the securities to cash. This process of price rises will continue until some security holders are willing to accept the new cash rather than keep the securities. Since the price on old securities moves inversely with the rate of interest, a rise in the price of securities is equivalent to a decrease in the interest rate. Only when the interest rate is already at the minimum will buyers prefer to hold the new money rather than offer any premium for securities.

Conversely, if there is a decrease in the amount of money available for passive balances, the security holders will try to replenish their cash supplies. To do so they will sell securities. Since such securities will find buyers only at a discount, the price will fall, thus increasing the rate of interest.

By the process outlined above, the prices of securities and interest rates will seesaw until someone is willing to hold the available stock of money. If there is too much money for which holders must be found at the going rate of interest, a game of "hot potato" ensues, with each participant trying to get rid of the excess money and acquire securities. This process continues until the interest rate is forced down enough to balance the demands for money and for securities. If there is too little money, all investors scramble for it until interest rates are driven up. All money will always be held, but only after interest rates have adjusted along the liquidity-preference curve will everyone be satisfied.

THE SUPPLY OF MONEY

Liquidity preference and transactions demand together constitute the demand for money. Equilibrium in the money market can come about only when this demand is equal to the available supply.

To discuss all the attributes of the money supply would require a complete analysis of the banking system. Such an analysis would take us far afield, into a general discussion of central banking and deposit creation by the banking system. These discussions are part of any course or textbook in money and banking. For our purposes, it is sufficient to state that the money supply may be taken as an exogenous variable, substantially under the control of the Treasury and the Federal Reserve System. We indicate the exogenous nature of the money supply by equation 3:

(3) $$M_s = M_0.$$

A further explanation of this approximation is given in the last section of this chapter.

THE MONEY EQUILIBRIUM CURVE

The essential condition for equilibrium in the money market is that the supply of money equal the demand for money. This can be stated as follows:

$$(4) \qquad\qquad M_s = M_1 + M_2.$$

With this condition, we are prepared to draw up the combinations of the rate of interest and the level of income that are consistent with equilibrium in the money market. The process is analogous to the derivation of the commodity equilibrium curve.

First we choose a level of income at random. From the transactions-demand function (equation 1), we know how much money (M_1) will be needed to finance this income. Since the supply of money is fixed at a level M_0 by equation 3, we can find the amount of money for passive balances by subtraction, since

$$(5) \qquad\qquad M_1 + M_2 = M_s = M_0.$$

When we have found such an amount of M_2, then the liquidity-preference function will tell us the resulting rate of interest. This rate of interest can be plotted against the original income level. By repeating the process, we derive other points. When we connect these points, we have a money equilibrium curve—that is, the curve of all combinations of the rate of interest and the level of income that are consistent with equilibrium in the money market.

Table 14 presents hypothetical data from which such a money equilibrium curve can be computed. Part A gives the

TABLE 14

DERIVATION OF A HYPOTHETICAL MONEY EQUILIBRIÚM CURVE
(Unit: one billion dollars)

Part A: Transactions Demand for Money		Part B: Money Demand Equals Money Supply*		Part C: Liquidity Preference	
Y	M_1	M_1	M_2	r	M_2
50	24	0	110	12%	5
100	45	10	100	10	11
150	63	30	80	8	20
200	78	50	60	6	32
250	90	70	40	4	47
300	99	90	20	2	65 or more
350	105	110	0		
400	108				

* Assuming $M_s = 110$.

transactions demand for money, corresponding to Figure 11. Part C gives the liquidity-preference function, corresponding to Figure 12. Part B merely expresses the equilibrium condition that the sum of the two demands must equal the money supply, in this case assumed to be 110 billion dollars. Other combinations could be added to this column.

Let us choose an income at random—say, 250 billion dollars. From the transactions demand (Part A), we find that this level will require 90 billion dollars of active balances. From Part B, we see that this will leave 20 billion dollars for idle holding. We would then expect, from the liquidity preference (Part C), that competition for this sum will drive the interest rate to 8 percent. This is one point on the money equilibrium curve.

Starting with a second income of 100 billion dollars, we find a required M_1 of 45 billion dollars. Interpolating on Part B, we find that 65 billion will be available for passive balances. From Part C, we find that this will push the interest rate down to 2 percent.

If we start with a 50-billion-dollar income, we find a required M_1 of 24 billion, leaving 86 billion for M_2. However, since the minimal interest rate of 2 percent has been reached, the interest rate will not go below this level.

TABLE 15

HYPOTHETICAL MONEY EQUILIBRIUM CURVE*
(Unit: one billion dollars)

Y	r
50	2%
100	2
150	4
200	
250	8
300	10
350	

* Derived from the data of Table 14.

These values, along with others, have been plotted in Table 15. The student should supply the remaining values.

The same kind of analysis can be shown in graphic form. Figure 14 applies the information given in Table 14 to the development of a money equilibrium curve. Choose an income at random—say 250 billion dollars. In Part A, we discover that this will require 90 billion dollars for transactions purposes. Part B is a 45-degree line downward, drawn so that the sum of M_1 and M_2 at every point is 110 billion dollars. From Part B, we find that there will be 20 billion dollars left for M_2. Entering Part C, we find that liquidity preference will force an interest rate of 8 percent. This interest rate is plotted in Part D against the 250-billion-dollar income with which we started. By repeating this process for other incomes, we derive other points on the money equilibrium curve. Again, the money equilibrium

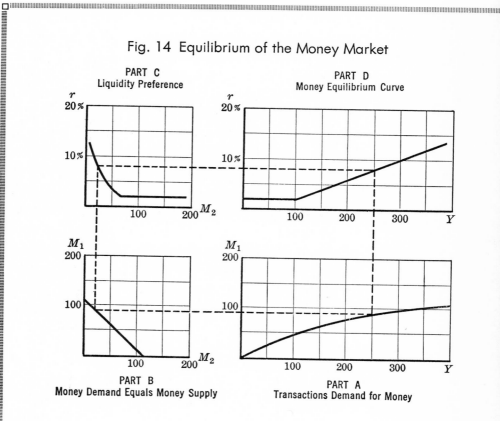

Fig. 14 Equilibrium of the Money Market

curve is obtained by finding the fourth corner of each of the rectangles drawn with corners on the three graphs representing transactions demand, money supply, and liquidity preference. The similarity of this derivation to that of the commodity equilibrium curve of Chapter 6 is clear.

BANKS AND LIQUIDITY PREFERENCE

This section explains, at least partly, the reason for accepting the money supply as completely exogenous. It is suggested that beginning students who are willing to accept this statement on faith skip this section and go on to Chapter 8.

The banking system can expand the money supply up to some multiple of the banks' reserves, the multiple being the inverse of the reserve ratio set by law or custom. In the United States, this ratio is fixed by law. If the banks always made all possible loans, control over the amount of reserves and the reserve ratio would result in complete control over the money supply. In fact, however, most American banks have excess reserves—that is, they usually do not make all the loans that they are permitted to make by law. When banks have these excess reserves, the monetary authorities do not have full control over the money supply, since an increase in reserves may mean only an increase in excess reserves rather than an increase in the money supply through new bank lending. The banks' reasons for keeping excess reserves are varied, but they are quite similar to the demand of individuals for idle balances. In situations in which an individual prefers idle cash, banks prefer excess reserves. The higher the rate of interest, the lower will be individuals' cash balances, and the lower will be banks' excess reserves. However, every dollar of bank excess reserves lowers the available money supply by several dollars, depending upon the required reserve ratio. If we wished to add together the liquidity-preference functions for individuals and banks, we should have to multiply the banks' excess reserves by this expansion factor in order to measure them in the same units as individuals' idle balances.

The actual supply of money depends upon the action of the monetary authorities and the preference of banks. The monetary authorities have complete control over the maximal potential money supply. If we define M_s as this potential rather than as the actual money supply, the liquidity-preference curve consists of two parts: the balances held by individuals, and the money balances which were never created because the banks chose to hold excess reserves instead. In this case, M_s is truly subject to complete political control, and the factors underlying $L(r)$ are unchanged. Since this more detailed description of the money supply is consistent with the system given earlier, the foregoing may be taken as justification for the outline which beginners are asked to accept on faith.

PROBLEMS AND DISCUSSION QUESTIONS

1. What effect would increased use of charge accounts have on the transactions demand for money? Can you suggest other factors that would shift the transactions demand?

2. If investors became generally more optimistic about the future, will the liquidity preference curve rise or fall? What other factors might cause changes in the curve?

3. The society requires, for transactions purposes, three months' income. The money supply is 120 billion dollars and the liquidity preference curve is as follows:

r	M_2
20%	20
15	40
10	70
5	100 or more

For these data, draw up the money equilibrium curve.

4. Using the data presented in problem 3, show the graphic derivation of the money equilibrium curve.

5. How would an increase in the money supply of 20 billion dollars affect the money equilibrium curve of problem 3?

SUGGESTED ADDITIONAL READINGS

Keynes discusses the demand for money in *The General Theory of Employment, Interest and Money*, Chapter 7. For a discussion of the empirical relevance of these concepts, see James Tobin, "Liquidity Preference and Monetary Policy," *Review of Economic Statistics*, 29:2 (May 1947), and the articles by Tobin and Clark Warburton in the same *Review*, 30:4 (November 1948).

For statistics of transactions in the United States, Morris A. Copeland, *A Study of Moneyflows in the United States* (New York: National Bureau of Economic Research, 1952).

CHAPTER 8

Equilibrium Income

I N CHAPTER 6, we derived the relationship between the rate of interest and the level of income that would provide equilibrium in the commodity market—the *commodity equilibrium curve*. In Chapter 7, the corresponding relationship in the money market was derived—the *money equilibrium curve*. The entire economy can be in equilibrium only if both these relationships are satisfied—that is, only if the final combination

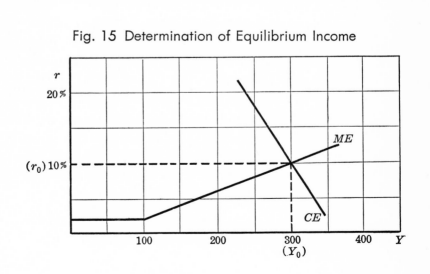

Fig. 15 Determination of Equilibrium Income

satisfies both these conditions. To find such a combination, we plot each of these curves as in Figure 15. Only the rate of interest r_0 and the national income Y_0 satisfy these conditions; therefore, Y_0 must be the equilibrium national income and r_0 the equilibrium rate of interest consistent with the exogenous variables studied previously.

Such a solution could be found numerically as well as graphically. Table 13 (p. 88) gave the commodity equilibrium curve for our assumed data; Table 15 (p. 106), the money equilibrium curve. These are combined in Table 16. From Table

TABLE 16

COMPUTATION OF EQUILIBRIUM INCOME
(Unit: one billion dollars)

Rate of Interest	*Income Which Produces Equilibrium in the Commodity Market**	*Income Which Produces Equilibrium in the Money Market†*
20%	240	
15	270	
12		400
10	300	300
8		250
6		200
5	330	
4		150
2		100

* From Table 13, page 88.
† From Table 15, page 106.

16, it is clear that both markets are satisfied only at an income of 300 billion dollars and an interest rate of 10 percent.

In order to understand the process by which the society moves to this equilibrium point, it will be necessary to revert to the basic data from which these functions were derived. Table 17 gives the derivation of both functions.

TABLE 17

DERIVATION OF COMMODITY EQUILIBRIUM CURVE
AND MONEY EQUILIBRIUM CURVE
(Unit: one billion dollars)

A. Commodity Equilibrium Curve*

(1)	(2)	(3)	(4)
r	I	S	Y
20%	5	30	240
15	15	40	270
10	25	50	300
5	35	60	330

* $G_0 = 25$ billion dollars.

B. Money Equilibrium Curve†

(5)	(6)	(7)	(8)
Y	M_1	M_2	r
50	24	86	2%
100	45	65	2
150	63	47	4
200	78	32	6
250	90	20	8
300	99	11	10
350	105	5	12

† $M_s = 110$ billion dollars.

Notice that columns 1 and 2 are the marginal-efficiency-of-capital schedule; columns 2 and 3, the equilibrium level of saving; columns 3 and 4, the saving function; and columns 1 and 4, the commodity equilibrium curve. Similarly, columns 5 and 6 are the transactions demand; 6 and 7, the equation of money supply and money demand; 7 and 8, the liquidity-preference schedule, and 5 and 8, the money equilibrium curve.

Let us examine the path of adjustment from a position which is not the equilibrium. Suppose we started at an income of 250 billion dollars and an interest rate of 8 percent. This position is consistent with equilibrium in the money market but not with equilibrium in the commodity market. Let us see the reaction by interpolating the necessary values. At an interest rate of 8 percent, business would invest about 29 billion dollars. This investment, coupled with the assumed constant government spending of 25 billion dollars, would require saving of 54 billion dollars and an expansion of income to 312 billion. With the interest rate at 8 percent, this level of income would be consistent with equilibrium in the commodity market, but the money market is now out of adjustment.

An income of 312 billion dollars would require about 100.4 billion dollars for transactions purposes, leaving 9.6 billion for M_2. Competition for this sum would drive interest rates to about $10\frac{1}{2}$ percent. The money market is now back in adjustment, but the commodity market must begin a new round of adjustment. This round would end with income at about 297 billion dollars. Further adjustments in the money market would lower the interest rate to about 9.9 percent. At this stage we may feel that we have come close enough to the final equilibrium values of 10 percent and 300 billion dollars. The purpose of following through this process of adjustment is to see the relation of this equilibrium value to the behavior of individuals in the society. This description is, obviously, very rigid in its summary of behavior, for the adjustments ordinarily take place simultaneously in both markets. Such simultaneous action will diminish the probability of fluctuations and permit the society to creep up on its equilibrium level.

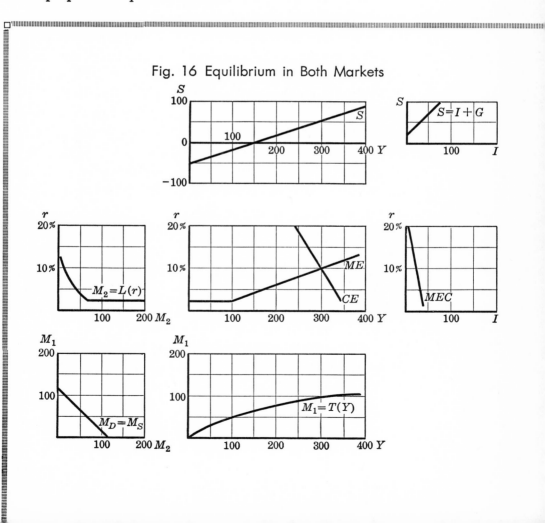

Fig. 16 Equilibrium in Both Markets

It is possible to combine the graphic derivations of the commodity equilibrium curve and the money equilibrium curve into one summary graph. The commodity equilibrium curve is the lower left-hand corner of Figure 10 (p. 89); the money equilibrium curve is the upper right-hand corner of Figure 14 (p. 107). These entire graphs can be superimposed, as shown in Figure 16. The four graphs in the upper right describe the commodity market; the four in the lower left, the money market.

THE MULTIPLIERS AGAIN

In Chapters 3 and 4, we computed various multipliers, each giving the reaction of national income to changes in government expenditures and other variables. Each of these multipliers assumed, however, that investment remained fixed at some previously determined level. The analysis of this chapter indicates that such an assumption is unrealistic. An increase in income would have repercussions in the money market, raising the rate of interest. This higher rate of interest would decrease the amount of investment and thereby keep income from rising as far as it otherwise would. If the money equilibrium curve were horizontal, the increase in income would not affect the interest rate. In such a case, the multiplier would give an accurate picture of the increase in income. In all other cases, the actual increase in income would be less than that given by the multiplier. Figure 17 indicates the difference between these shifts. CE' represents the new commodity equilibrium curve after an increase in government spending.

AN EXAMPLE: INCREASED GOVERNMENT SPENDING

As an indication of the repercussions that would take place throughout the economy as the result of a change in one factor, let us examine the effect of increased government expenditures. Let us assume that government expenditures increase by 21 billion dollars. The multiplier being three, the commodity equilibrium curve moves to the right 63 billion dollars. This new commodity equilibrium curve intersects the money equilibrium curve at an income of 350 billion dollars and an interest rate of 12 percent. Such a shift is illustrated in Figure 18.

From an examination of the new equilibrium position, we see that investment has fallen from 25 to 21 billion dollars,

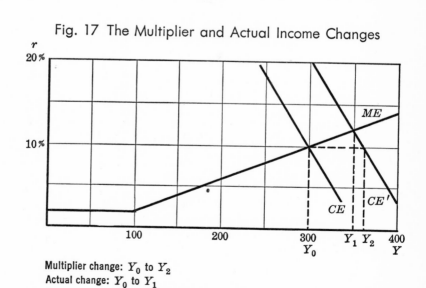

Fig. 17 The Multiplier and Actual Income Changes

Multiplier change: Y_0 to Y_2
Actual change: Y_0 to Y_1
Dampening effect of change in interest rate: Y_2 to Y_1

government spending has risen from 25 to 46 billion dollars, and saving has risen from 50 to 67 billion dollars. In the money market, we see that the money supply has been reallocated, with 105 billion dollars used for transactions (M_1) and five billion for liquidity (M_2), as compared with the previous values of 99 billion and 11 billion dollars, respectively.

The student should test his understanding of this process by examining the effects of changes in all the basic functions

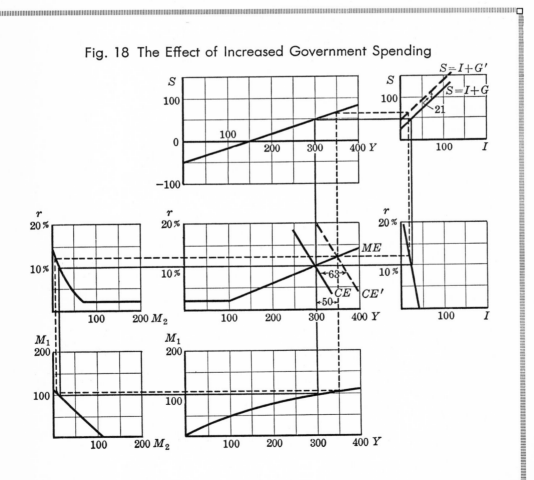

Fig. 18 The Effect of Increased Government Spending

on the rate of interest, income, saving, investment, active balances, and passive balances. He should be prepared to discuss the effect of an increase (or decrease) in the marginal efficiency of capital, government spending, the saving function, liquidity preference, the transactions demand, and the supply of money. Note in each case that we are discussing the effects of *shifts* in curves, not movements along the curves.

The effect of changes in taxes can also be analyzed in these terms. A change in tax has the same effect as a change in saving. This can be shown in detail by substituting the saving-plus-tax function of Figure 7 (p. 65) for the saving function of Figure 16.

PROBLEMS

1. Using the data of problems 1, Chapter 6 (p. 91), and 3, Chapter 7 (p. 110), find the equilibrium income and interest rate. Find the equilibrium values of I, S, M_1, and M_2.

2. Using the same data, find the effect of an increase in the money supply to 170 billion dollars. What would be the new equilibrium values of r, Y, I, S, M_1, and M_2?

CHAPTER 9

Investment

I N CHAPTER 5, we discussed a rather simplified model of the investment process. According to that analysis, businessmen will make an investment if the marginal efficiency of capital exceeds the rate of interest. The marginal efficiency of capital is the rate of return that makes the purchase price equal to the present value of the expected net returns. These future returns are obtained by subtracting future costs from future gross revenues. Therefore, the marginal efficiency of capital can be altered by any factor that changes one of the three components: purchase price, future revenues, and future costs.

It must be remembered that we are considering factors that change the marginal efficiency of a specific investment or of all investments. We will therefore examine those forces that tend to shift the marginal-efficiency-of-capital schedule. Each of the factors discussed in this chapter will cause a shift in the schedule; that is, either more or less investment will be worth while at a given rate of interest. Since we are concerned only with the schedule itself, we will not discuss the interest rate. Changes in the rate of interest cause movements *along* the schedule; the changes discussed here cause shifts *of* the schedule itself.

EXPECTATIONS AND INVESTMENT

Two of the three items used in computing the marginal-efficiency-of-capital schedule are future costs and future revenues. Since these items can seldom be determined objectively, the expectations of businessmen for the future are very important. If businessmen feel generally optimistic, they will estimate future revenues high and future costs low, with a correspondingly high marginal efficiency of capital. If they feel pessimistic, the marginal efficiency of capital will be low. This influence is so important that entire theories of income variation have been built upon "waves of optimism and pessimism." Occasionally some astrologer-turned-economist chooses to find a relation between these moods and cosmic rays, sunspots, or other radiations from outer space. Novelists sometimes give the impression that these attitudes (and the expectations derived from them) stem from the businessman's reaction to a case of indigestion or to a pleasant smile from his wife at the breakfast table. Such economic studies of the investment process as are available indicate that most business expectations are made of much more substantial stuff. They result from engineering studies, market surveys, analysis of economic trends, and other such research. The importance of such research as compared with subjective factors has been indicated on several occasions, when executive opinion surveys reported that the average businessman expected a general recession but that he was still planning new investments "because our firm is different." Apparently the research data for his firm influenced his decisions more than his impressions of the economy. Investment decisions have not yet been reduced to a simple routine within the capabilities of ordinary clerks, but they are far removed from the area of whim and superstition.

Any analysis of the future usually starts with the conditions of the present. In the absence of any concrete evidence that a change should be expected, businessmen will assume that the conditions of the present will continue into the future. This statement is, of course, obvious, but it underscores the fact that changes will determine the *deviations from the present*. Thus, a businessman who is trying to estimate his future labor costs must begin with a knowledge of the labor-union strength in his firm, in his industry, and in the country at large. From these data, he can estimate whether or not the general trend of wages in his firm will be similar to that in the rest of the country. Similarly, if he is trying to estimate the tax costs for his firm, he will generally start with the present level of taxes and modify this level by prospective changes in the structure.

It is also worth while to remind ourselves that the future returns involved cover a series of time periods in the future. Equation 9 of Chapter 5 told us that the marginal efficiency of capital is the yield (r) which makes

$$(1) \qquad Q = \frac{R_1}{1+r} + \frac{R_2}{(1+r)^2} + \frac{R_3}{(1+r)^3} + \ldots + \frac{R_n}{(1+r)^n},$$

assuming Q to be the purchase price and R_1, R_2, R_3, ... R_n the returns in successive years. It is therefore clear that the result if a given change affects only one term—say, R_3—is quite different from the result if the change affects them all. In casual economic analysis, there is often a tendency to assume that all R's are identical and that any factor that affects one R affects all.

An example will make this distinction clearer. In 1953, Congress extended the excess-profits tax on corporations for one year. The tax duly expired on January 1, 1954. At the time of the extension, dire results were predicted on the ground that this tax lowered returns so much that investment would be unprofitable. Such an assumption was probably unwarranted. Even if an investment could be made with no time lag, only the first year's return would be affected by the tax. On a 20-year investment which yields 8 percent, cutting the first year's return to *zero* would lower the yield only to 7 percent. Since the tax did not erase the return completely, this change is an overestimate of its effects. If the investment took some time in construction, the tax extension might expire without altering any of the returns, for the new investment might not produce before January 1, 1954.

In view of the rather slight effects indicated above, why were there such catastrophic predictions? One might attribute the argument to pure propaganda or to businessmen's traditional dislike for taxes. More probably, the answer lies in the failure to distinguish between a decline in R_1, the return for the first year, and all the R's of the stream. It is true that a permanent extension of the excess-profits tax would have caused a substantial decline in the marginal efficiency of capital; it is not true that a short temporary extension would have that effect.

In fairness to the opponents of this tax, there is one important argument against even a temporary extension. Businessmen might feel that a temporary extension could be followed by another temporary extension and thus become, in fact, permanent. Looking back, we can see that the congressmen who voted for the extension had no such intention. But businessmen are not mind readers. They must guess the intention from the action and might infer an intention to make the tax permanent. If the extension creates such an expectation among businessmen, then, in fact, all R's are lowered, and the predicted results occur.

The succeeding sections of this chapter discuss some of the elements that affect these expectations, as well as certain other factors affecting the marginal efficiency of capital. These objective factors do not, however, explain everything. There always remains a degree of uncertainty stemming from the estimation of some uncontrolled variables. The uncertainty about the permanence of the tax extension discussed above is one such case, but there are many others. These uncertainties explain the popularity among businessmen of those periodicals that claim to predict future trends. It also explains the increasing competition among "Washington newsletters," which concentrate on government developments. These uncertainties also account for the fact that the analysis of investment is one of the least satisfactory aspects of economic theory.

INNOVATION

New techniques, processes, and products have always been important stimuli to investment. Many business-cycle theories have placed their main emphasis on the role which these new developments have played in promoting investment. An innovation is the introduction of any of these new elements into the economic process. It therefore usually requires investment, because processes and techniques are often built into the capital structure of a plant. (Imagine trying production-line assembly of automobiles in a commercial garage, or custom building on an assembly line.) In many cases, a new product requires new machinery for processing it. Thus, innovation and investment usually go hand in hand.

The impetus to such investment can be traced to the lowering of costs or the increase in revenues. Unless a new product produces more revenue than any of the existing products, it remains merely an invention, one more model and set of plans to clutter the files of the U.S. Patent Office. Only when the prospective revenue from a new product is high does the invention find its way into the economic process and become an innovation. Similarly, new production techniques are adopted only if they are more efficient and therefore cheaper than existing methods. Thus, we can say that the marginal efficiency of capital is increased by a steady flow of new innovations.

The foregoing summary presents only half the picture. It is true that innovation increases the marginal efficiency of capital for the innovator. It is also true that it causes the marginal efficiency of capital to fall for the older firms. (Imagine what must have happened to the marginal efficiency of capital in the buggy industry during the early years of the twentieth century.) In some cases, the fear of competition from products yet unborn may decrease the marginal efficiency. If a given industry has a record of innovation which demonstrates that new developments will make the old methods obsolete about every five years, then a firm contemplating a new investment might well set R_6, R_7, etc. all equal to zero, indicating that it can expect nothing after the fifth year. Such circumstances might actually lower the marginal efficiency.

The net effect of these two forces is usually in the direction of a higher marginal efficiency of capital. Since the depressing effect on older firms will not take place unless the investment is made in the innovating firm, it is clear that there must be at least some force in the direction of a higher marginal efficiency. Sometimes this effect will appear without disturbing other firms. Only in the case of capital-saving innovations will the net effect be a decrease. In such a case, the investment that is foregone might be greater than the investment that is made. But even this effect is not inevitable, for it might be possible to continue the older process with old capital. Even if the innovation uses less capital per unit of output, whatever capital is used must be *new* capital (investment), whereas the older techniques might be able to continue with older equipment. Thus, we may be reasonably confident that innovation increases the marginal efficiency of capital.

OLD CAPITAL AND NEW INVESTMENT

Just as innovation may have a depressing effect on expansion of older methods, so the existence of old capital depresses the marginal efficiency for new investments. Other things being equal, the more capital in existence, the lower the marginal efficiency of capital. This is true because the old capital has presumably been invested in the most profitable enterprises, leaving the poorer ones unexploited. The heavy-traffic railroads have been built, leaving less profitable spur lines for the future. The existing firms in the automobile industry blanket quite well the range of consumer preferences, leaving only the luxury custom business or the low-priced small car for the newcomer.

Lest this sound too much like the complaint of Alexander the Great that there are no new worlds to conquer, let us hasten to add that other things are never equal. In the process of building an industry, all the good opportunities within that industry may be exploited, but often entire new industries are developed to complement it. No large railroads have been built in the United States in the twentieth century; the nineteenth century built them all. But many twentieth-century factories have been built because the nineteenth-century railroads provided suitable transportation facilities. Similarly, the automobile industry has no need for another General Motors; the society, however, needs good turnpike builders. Although many good opportunities have already been pre-empted in societies like the United States—more than in societies like India—unexplored projects still exist for future development. This is partly because there are more investment avenues to be explored in an industrial society and partly because the act of growth engenders more possibilities of growth. Our continued investment in the past has built up our capital-goods industries, which are themselves outlets for investment.

Despite the fact that progress begets progress, there are some economists who maintain that we have about reached our limit in exploiting new areas of production and must content ourselves with multiplying and improving the old. Whether or not they are correct only time can tell. If they are, we can expect a lower rate of investment. An old machine will be replaced with a better one only if all costs (fixed and variable) for the new machine are less than the variable costs of the old one. Since the fixed costs of the old machine continue whether the machine is used or not, they can be ignored in making decisions about replacements. Firms with fleets of cars and trucks usually replace them when the maintenance of the old vehicles is more expensive than the cost of purchasing new ones.

If our society is nearing the stage in which all new investment must compete directly with old capital, we should expect the marginal efficiency to be relatively low. The facts of the case are still quite uncertain.

NATIONAL GROWTH

As a society expands, its markets expand with it. Such expansion, of course, leads to an increase in expected revenues, which, in turn, causes a rise in the marginal efficiency of capital. Thus, population growth and the development of new territories were an important factor in the high marginal efficiency of capital in the United States in the nineteenth century. Similarly, the increase in births in the United States during the 1940's has been hailed as an insurance against depression, for it causes an increase in the marginal efficiency of capital.

We have already noted the importance of innovation in increasing the marginal efficiency of capital. Most investments, however, represent not innovations but, rather, expansion of facilities already in existence. It is important to exploit new processes and techniques—to produce electricity from atomic energy, gasoline from shale, and steel from low-grade iron ore. Quantitatively, these innovations are overshadowed by simple expansion—more steel mills, more Diesel locomotives, more oil refineries. Probably the most important single factor in the expansion of these older forms of investment is the general expansion of markets in a growing society.

In the past, population growth increased the marginal efficiency of capital in another way: through its effect on expected future costs. An expanding population increases the labor supply, with a normal tendency to depress wages. Lower expected labor costs, by increasing expected net returns, increase the marginal efficiency of capital. Such factors may have been important in the nineteenth century, when immigration and a high birth rate were swelling our population. Their importance in the United States of the twentieth century is lessened by decreased immigration and by increased unionization. The effect is mentioned here only as a sidelight on economic history.

STAGNATION

The decade of the thirties was a period of widespread unemployment in most countries. In the United States and England, many economists considered this unemployment a sign of vanishing investment opportunity. They argued that most of the best opportunities had already been exploited and that investment would not be sufficient to guarantee full employment. As a solution, they proposed that the government undertake a long-run policy of deficit spending to ensure full use of our resources. They also suggested certain programs to increase the consumption function, in order to reduce the amount of intended saving.

This argument had several facets. The first was the passing of the frontier. There no longer were any uninhabited territories to be settled and developed. The United States had less need for railroads and the purely physical marketing facilities which make settlements into towns and territories into states. Secondly, it seemed that the population of the United States would increase more slowly in the future. Throughout the twenties and thirties, although the population was still rising, the birth rate fell steadily. There would consequently be less need for *addi-*

tional housing and *additional* facilities to produce consumer goods, although the replacement demand would continue. Finally, the nineteenth and early twentieth centuries were periods of unprecedented technological change. Railroads, petroleum, steel, chemicals, automobiles, and electrical equipment were among the industries which grew during this period. There were grave doubts that such a pace could be maintained, much less exceeded. Since the other factors indicated less investment, technological change must provide all the more opportunities for investment and there was no evidence that it would do so.

The arguments for and against the stagnation thesis raged without any solution. A precise answer is impossible, by the nature of the problem, for this is economic "crystal-ball gazing" of the greatest magnitude. Even now, more than twenty years later, it is difficult to come to any firm conclusion. The "baby boom" has ruled out the population argument; the territorial argument remains intact. Technological progress continues, but comparison of rates is very unprecise. The history of the years since 1946 can be cited on both sides. Stagnationists point out that we have maintained full employment only by large-scale government spending. It is true that the spending was undertaken for other reasons, but it is probable that there would have been unemployment without it. The decline in employment in 1954 occurred despite a very large government budget. The Eisenhower proposal for a huge highway program has been cited as evidence that he has joined the ranks of the stagnationists. Opponents charge that private investment and consumption would have filled the gap if it had not been for the depressive effects of the high taxes which were required by the large government programs. The argument continues, and the outcome remains in doubt.

PURCHASE PRICE

The marginal efficiency of capital equates the present value of expected returns with the purchase price of the new investment goods. All the factors which we have been discussing affect the expected returns; the time has now come to consider the purchase price.

Unlike future revenues, the purchase price has an objective reality. It can be obtained either by consulting a catalog or by asking contractors for bids. It is therefore not subject to whims of the estimator but is the reflection of cost and market conditions in the capital-goods industries.

Every technical advance in the capital-goods industries increases the marginal efficiency of capital in other industries. Similarly, increases in costs in the capital-goods industries lower the marginal efficiency of capital in all other industries. This relationship explains at least partly the great interest throughout the society in the wage negotiations of the steel industry and in the depletion of our iron mines.

Capital-goods industries are not exempt from the law of diminishing returns. If the demand for investment goods is very high, capital-goods firms will be working near capacity levels. As this level of operations is reached, inefficiencies creep in, and costs rise. Therefore, the marginal efficiency of capital, which is a demand for investment, is lowered when a high level of investment actually takes place.

In addition to the purely technical cost factors in the capital-goods industries, the degree of competition is also quite important. The greater degree of monopoly there is in an industry, the higher will be the actual purchase price of capital goods. Such market monopoly in the capital-goods area is probably less dangerous than it would be in a consumer industry. Most of the firms that buy investment goods are well informed on possible alternative sources of supply; many of them are large. enough to provide such alternatives themselves. In such a case, the competitiveness of the market is measured not by the number of firms but by all the *potential* alternatives.

GOVERNMENT AND INVESTMENT

In the modern world, no form of economic activity escapes the influence of government. The marginal efficiency of capital is affected by many forms of government activity.

The most obvious influence is through taxation. Higher taxes either increase costs or decrease revenues, in both cases lowering the marginal efficiency of capital. Sales taxes lead to lower gross revenue, payroll and property taxes to increased costs. Corporation income taxes reduce directly the net return, the difference between revenues and costs. Even personal income taxes have their effect on the marginal efficiency, for they reduce sales and therefore diminish expected revenues.

There is one form of taxation that would not have such

adverse effects upon investment. This would be a tax on pure economic profit—that is, a tax on the return above all costs, both explicit and implicit. Such a tax would be so designed as to lower the marginal efficiency of any profitable investment to a point just above the going rate of interest. For example, if the current rate of interest were 6 percent and a given investment, after allowance for risk, yielded 10 percent, the projected tax would reduce the yield on this investment *almost* to 6 percent. In such a case, the level of investment would not be affected. Unfortunately, such a tax is not possible administratively. No one has ever been able to construct a tax that is capable of objective determination and that lowers the yield on 10-percent investments to 6 percent without at the same time lowering the yield on 7-percent investments to 5 percent. All our present "profits" taxes are levied in part upon elements that are in actuality costs. The present corporate income tax, for example, does not allow deduction of interest on the money provided by stockholders. We may therefore regard all present taxes as lowering, in varying degree, the marginal efficiency of capital.

The influence of government on the marginal efficiency does not end with taxes. Government expenditures can have an important effect. If these expenditures are apt to be competitive with business output, expected revenues and the marginal efficiency will decline; if the expenditures are complementary, expected revenues and the marginal efficiency will increase. Many government projects may have both effects. For example, the electricity program of the Tennessee Valley Authority lowered the marginal efficiency of capital for private utilities in the area but raised it for appliance dealers. Many other firms found a higher marginal efficiency of capital because their expected power costs declined. Most government activities are of this type, increasing the marginal efficiency for some firms and lowering it for others.

Even government transfer payments may affect the marginal efficiency of capital. Unemployment-compensation payments tend to make workers less willing to accept low wages. Therefore, such payments raise labor costs and decrease the marginal efficiency of capital. (Nineteenth-century economists opposed the British poor laws along lines of reasoning similar to the above, thus helping to earn for economics its title of "the dismal science.")

The regulatory activities of the government also have their effect. Vigorous anti-trust action will lower the marginal efficiency of capital for firms affected, since in fighting the case, even successfully, they might suffer a decrease in revenues or an increase in costs. Such action might, however, break down barriers to entry into the industry, thus raising the marginal efficiency for new firms. Protective tariffs raise the marginal efficiency for the protected firms but lower it for firms which use the imported goods.

The general tenor of the administration may also have its effect on the marginal efficiency of capital. If businessmen feel that a certain administration is unfriendly to business, they may lower their estimates of future returns on the ground that the government will find some way to make the project unprofitable. If businessmen expect the government to go completely socialist in five years, they will have lower expectations of future revenues (zero for the sixth and succeeding years). As is so often the case with expectations, it does not matter whether these political predictions are correct or not, for unrealistic expectations decrease investment just as much as realistic ones.

The generally increased importance of government in the economic life of the nation is reflected by the increased attention paid to politics in business periodicals. As recently as 1932, *Business Week* made only occasional comments on the presidential elections. In 1952, it provided detailed coverage of the campaign and the speeches of the candidates. Similar changes have been evident in the coverage of other business periodicals.

CAPITAL RATIONING

Many economists have pointed out that investments are often stifled because funds are unavailable rather than because capital charges are too high. In such cases, a firm may find that banks and other lenders quote an interest rate of, say, 7 percent but state that they have no money to lend. (Such a situation faced many veterans in the early 1950's, when the interest rate on guaranteed mortgages was 4 percent, as provided by law, but no lenders were taking such mortgages.) Actually, of course, the situation never reaches a point at which no loans are being made, but, at certain times, borrowers may be screened with especial care. At such times as these, banks are accused of refusing to lend money unless the prospective borrower can prove that he does not need it. Thus we have a case of informal rationing rather than a rise in interest rates.

This rationing is more apparent than real. In Chapter 5, we noted that the market rate of interest includes factors other than the pure rate of interest. One of the most important of these factors is risk. At a time when the federal government may be paying 2 percent on loans of a given period, businesses may be paying 6 percent, indicating a risk premium of 4 percent (government loans are presumably riskless). If a lender chose to screen applicants very carefully, he could cut the risk to, say, 3 percent. To this selected group he could then lend at a market rate of 5 percent (2-percent interest plus 3-percent risk).

In the case of "capital rationing" discussed above, the lender increases his scrutiny of prospective borrowers but does not change the market rate of interest. But in effect, this increased scrutiny constitutes a rise in the pure interest rate, for every decrease in risk means an increase in the pure rate.

Many of the alleged cases of capital rationing are, rather, matters of a difference of opinion between the borrower and the lender on appropriate risk premiums. A firm that wishes to sell bonds to, say, an insurance company can almost always do so if it will accept a suitable discount. This discount is merely a device for converting a 6-percent bond to 8 percent or more. Often the borrower will refuse to accept such a discount, especially if a rival firm has managed to sell its bonds without discount. Although the borrower may feel that this is a case of capital rationing, to the lender it is merely a case of a market rate of interest's being too low to cover the pure rate plus a suitable risk premium. The appropriate risk premium is always determined by the lender. There is, however, ample evidence that lenders sometimes determine this premium on the basis of "goodwill," friendship, and even caprice. This discrimination among borrowers was one of the principal arguments for establishing government lending programs, especially for agriculture and for new firms.

We may therefore regard so-called cases of capital rationing as instances in which the marginal efficiency of the investment is too low to cover the risk plus the rate of interest. "Loans to selected borrowers" is merely one way to cover a rise in interest rates.

THE ACCELERATOR

In business-cycle literature, it is common to emphasize the principle of the accelerator. This principle states that new investment tends to be proportional to the change in consumption (or income). A numerical example will make this concept clear. Let us suppose that machines of a certain type turn out 100 units of product per day and that current production is 10,000 units per day. Then 100 machines will be required. If the machines last for 20 years, the normal replacement demand for these machines will be five machines per year.

Let us assume that next year the demand for this product increases by 10 percent. This means 11,000 units of product per day, requiring 110 machines. Therefore, in addition to the usual replacement demand of five machines, there will be a demand for

10 new machines to handle the additional demand for 1,000 units. Thus, a 10-percent increase in demand can cause a 200-percent increase in investment. If demand had remained the same, investment would have been only for replacement. Thus, the accelerator places the emphasis on these changes in demand, not on their absolute level.

This theory is rather appealing, but an examination of the necessary conditions indicates that it is not very realistic. First of all, it assumes that there must be no unused capacity. If the firm described above already had 120 machines and were using only 100, one would not expect any increase in investment from a modest increase in demand. Therefore, the accelerator will not operate in a depression, which is characterized by excess capacity. Secondly, the accelerator assumes a fixed ratio between capital and output. This assumption is occasionally justified, but most firms can substitute labor for capital, at least within a limited range. Therefore, the investment process is more complicated than is indicated by the accelerator. Finally, even if these other conditions are fulfilled, businesses will purchase the new machines only if the demand is expected to remain high for the life of the machine. We have already mentioned some of the difficulties that arise when the first year's return (R_1) is used as the basis for determining the return for all later years. To imagine that businessmen always make this simple assumption is to attribute to them a degree of naïveté that few of them possess.

For those who prefer empirical proof or disproof of these principles, we may say that the attempted statistical demonstrations of the accelerator have been remarkably unconvincing.

Even though we reject the simple version of the accelerator, it does afford a clue to certain features of the investment process. Given the amount of old capital in existence, a rising national income tends to mean a higher marginal efficiency of capital; a declining national income tends to mean a low marginal efficiency.

TYPES OF INVESTMENT

The Department of Commerce separates private domestic capital formation into three categories: new construction, producers' durable equipment, and net change in business inventories. Figure 19 indicates the course of investment and its components in recent years. Each of these components is subject to its own peculiarities and is worthy of brief comment.

Construction is of two kinds, residential and commercial. Commercial construction is subject to almost the same influences as producers' durable equipment and will therefore be discussed in the section on durable equipment. Residential construction seems to depend mostly upon the growth of the society and the stock of old buildings. The demand for housing space is relatively stable, changing mainly with population and family structure. The stock of old houses is the result of past building less the losses caused by wear and tear. Although one would expect such conditions to make residential construction a relatively stable component of investment, this has not been the case. The housing industry is characterized by a multitude of small

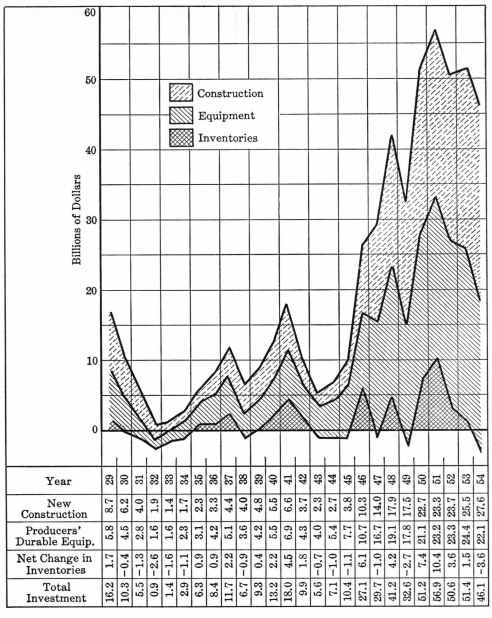

Year	29	30	31	32	33	34	35	36	37	38	39	40	41	42	43	44	45	46	47	48	49	50	51	52	53	54
New Construction	8.7	6.2	4.0	1.9	1.4	1.7	2.3	3.3	4.4	4.0	4.8	5.5	6.6	3.7	2.3	2.7	3.8	10.3	14.0	17.9	17.5	22.7	23.3	23.7	25.5	27.6
Producers' Durable Equip.	5.8	4.5	2.8	1.6	1.6	2.3	3.1	4.2	5.1	3.6	4.2	5.5	6.9	4.3	4.0	5.4	7.7	10.7	16.7	19.1	17.8	21.1	23.2	23.3	24.4	22.1
Net Change in Inventories	1.7	−0.4	−1.3	−2.6	−1.6	−1.1	0.9	0.9	2.2	−0.9	0.4	2.2	4.5	1.8	−0.7	−1.0	−1.1	6.1	−1.0	4.2	−2.7	7.4	10.4	3.6	1.5	−3.6
Total Investment	16.2	10.3	5.5	0.9	1.4	2.9	6.3	8.4	11.7	6.7	9.3	13.2	18.0	9.9	5.6	7.1	10.4	27.1	29.7	41.2	32.6	51.2	56.9	50.6	51.4	46.1

Fig. 19 Investment and Its Components*

* From *Survey of Current Business, National Income Supplement 1954*, pp. 162–163.

contractors. The number grows in good times and falls off in poor times. The fragmentation of housing "manufacture" customarily results in overbuilding during housing booms, which overbuilding results, in turn, in depressed rents and selling prices and, consequently, in few new homes being built. During the lean years, many contractors drop out and many building-trades workmen shift to other industries. Gradually the depreciation of older homes and the growth of population creates a condition of higher prices and higher rents. Since it takes time to reorganize the industry, the demand usually becomes acute before it is met. Then the process starts over again.

If the supply of, and the demand for residential housing had originally been equal, they might have continued to be so. Boom construction tends to repeat itself, and the bunching in age distribution of houses will tend to mean a bunching of replacement needs. In the United States, the cycle from boom to boom customarily lasts about 17 years, although one might imagine a situation in which new construction methods (and a change in the durability of houses) could alter this time span.

Certain government activities have been undertaken to simplify the financing of home construction, notably under the Federal Housing Administration and, for veterans, under the so-called G.I. Bill of Rights. These programs involve government insurance of the loan so as to reduce the risk to the lender. These reductions of risk have effectively lowered the market rate of interest and made buyers eligible for mortgage credit. In this manner, they have greatly reduced "capital rationing" in the construction field.

Producers' durable equipment refers mainly to machinery. If we include commercial construction in the consideration of durable equipment, we have plant and equipment for manufacturing, store and fixtures for retailing. These investments are more than all other investments combined and are closely related to the fluctuations of the national income which have come to be known as the "business cycle." They are subject to all the influences which have been discussed in this chapter.

Business inventories may change in either direction. In the analysis of these changes, the accelerator principle has perhaps its greatest usefulness. Most businesses prefer to maintain a fairly constant ratio between sales and inventories. Since these inventories can be sold off rather rapidly, there are seldom excess inventories for any long period of time. Because inventories are turned over within a relatively short period of time, no extended series of expected returns appears but only the expected return when they are sold (soon). Thus, all the conditions for the application of the accelerator are met. The relatively short turnover and relative changeability of inventories leads to a short inventory cycle, usually about 40 months.

A second factor which is very important, especially in the analysis of raw-materials inventories, is expected change in the price level. In previous chapters, however, we have not been considering changes in price levels. We therefore leave this topic for later treatment.

DISCUSSION QUESTIONS

1. What factors induce a firm to undertake innovation? What are the difficulties in a pure profit calculation?

2. Many decisions on investment are made by hired managers who are interested in their own salaries and power rather than in the profits of stockholders. What effect can this difference in concern have upon investment?

3. What do you think are the prospects for stagnation of investment?

4. How would investment be affected by the fact that businesses have motivations other than profit?

5. Summarize the procedure that you would suggest a large corporation use in making its investment decisions.

SUGGESTED ADDITIONAL READINGS

An analysis of the techniques of decision making is presented by Walter W. Heller in "The Anatomy of Investment Decisions," *Harvard Business Review*, March 1951, and by George Katona, in "Psychological Analysis of Business Decisions and Expectations," *American Economic Review*, Vol. 36, 1946.

The role of innovations has been especially emphasized by Joseph A. Schumpeter in *The Theory of Economic Development* (Cambridge, Mass.: Harvard University Press, 1934). See also Oscar Lange, "A Note on Innovations," *Review of Economic Statistics*, February 1943.

The leading proponent of the stagnation thesis in this country is Alvin M. Hansen. See especially his "Economic Progress and Declining Population Growth," *American Economic Review*, 29:1, (March 1939), reprinted in *Readings in*

Business Cycle Theory (Philadelphia: Blakiston, 1944), and his view 13 years later in Heller, Boddy, and Nelson (eds.), *Savings in the Modern Economy* (Minneapolis: University of Minnesota Press, 1953), Chapter 4. Against this theory, compare the views of George Terborgh, *The Bogey of Economic Maturity* (Chicago: Machinery and Allied Products Institute, 1945), and David McCord Wright, in *Savings in the Modern Economy*, Chapter 13.

The accelerator principle was originally stated by J. M. Clark in "Business Acceleration and the Law of Demand," *Journal of Political Economy*, 1917, reprinted in *Readings in Business Cycle Theory*.

CHAPTER 10

Consumption

I N CHAPTER 3, we discussed a simple consumption function, in
which income was the only determinant of consumption. In
Chapter 4, we modified this function slightly, by suggesting
that it was disposable income, or take-home-pay, that was really
significant in determining consumption. Neither of these descrip-
tions is complete. Although income (or disposable income) may
be the most important *single* variable in determining the level
of consumption, many other factors are relevant. Some of these
other factors are discussed in this chapter. We shall discuss
first the factors that influence individual behavior and then summarize these factors to construct a consumption function for the
society.

TYPES OF CONSUMPTION

In the national-income statistics of the Department of Commerce consumption goods are classified in two different ways.

The first classification groups these goods according to the type of expenditure they represent, such as food, clothing, etc. For some detailed analyses, this grouping is very useful. In attempting an over-all survey, it is usually more profitable to classify goods according to the type of product—that is, durable goods, non-durable goods, and services. Figure 20 illustrates the changes in consumption over the years.

These product divisions are not completely precise. Ordinarily, one would say that a television set is a durable good and that television repair is a service. But if the set is sold with a one-year guarantee, the entire cost is usually subsumed under the classification of a durable good, although it is clear that a portion of the payment reimburses the seller for the expected cost of repairs. We should therefore regard this method of classification as an approximate one. None of the discussion in this chapter will assume any great precision in this type of grouping.

For purposes of economic analysis, the most important distinction is between durable goods on the one hand and non-durable goods and services on the other. For the latter group, the purchase and the actual use of the goods is almost simultaneous. The time elapsed between purchasing a ticket and seeing a play or motion picture may be only a matter of minutes and is seldom more than a few days. Similarly, most foods are purchased for use within a week or two at most.

Durable goods are of a different type, for they are used for many years after their purchase. This range of time between purchase and use causes many problems. In Chapter 2 we discussed the problem it raises for statisticians: Should con-

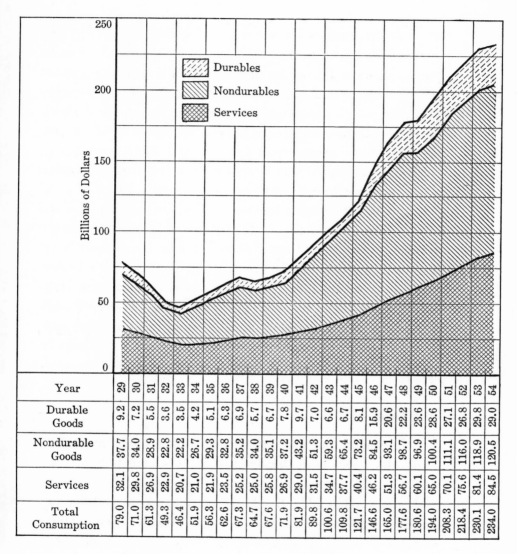

Year	29	30	31	32	33	34	35	36	37	38	39	40	41	42	43	44	45	46	47	48	49	50	51	52	53	54
Durable Goods	9.2	7.2	5.5	3.6	3.5	4.2	5.1	6.3	6.9	5.7	6.7	7.8	9.7	7.0	6.6	6.7	8.1	15.9	20.6	22.2	23.6	28.6	27.1	26.8	29.8	29.0
Nondurable Goods	37.7	34.0	28.9	22.8	22.2	26.7	29.3	32.8	35.2	34.0	35.1	37.2	43.2	51.3	59.3	65.4	73.2	84.5	93.1	98.7	96.9	100.4	111.1	116.0	118.9	120.5
Services	32.1	29.8	26.9	22.9	20.7	21.0	21.9	23.5	25.2	25.0	25.8	26.9	29.0	31.5	34.7	37.7	40.4	46.2	51.3	56.7	60.1	65.0	70.1	75.6	81.4	84.5
Total Consumption	79.0	71.0	61.3	49.3	46.4	51.9	56.3	62.6	67.3	64.7	67.6	71.9	81.9	89.8	100.6	109.8	121.7	146.6	165.0	177.6	180.6	194.0	208.3	218.4	230.1	234.0

Fig. 20 Consumption and Its Components*

* From *Survey of Current Business, National Income Supplement 1954*, pp. 162–163.

sumption be measured at the time of purchase or at use? The statisticians agreed to base their measurements on the time of purchase, since that is the time at which income is produced for the seller. It is also, in any case, the easiest time to measure. (Only for houses does the treatment differ. Since there is a well-developed rental market for houses, all purchases of houses are treated as investment, and their rental value is treated as consumption. For owner-occupied houses, this means imputing a fictitious rental payment by the owner to himself.)

For the analysis of national income, the statisticians' decision is the correct one. The influence of a purchase on the economy comes at the time of purchase. Even if the buyer keeps his new refrigerator in the crate, businesses have made profits, workers have been hired, and materials have been used. However, we cannot ignore these goods once they have been sold. One of the important factors in determining sales of such goods is the stock already in the hands of consumers. We will therefore give especial attention to these goods.

DURABLE ASSETS

In general, one may say that the existence of a large stock of durable goods in the hands of consumers tends to lessen consumption. The more durable goods one owns, the fewer he wishes to purchase. We should therefore expect to find that two families with exactly the same income but with different stocks of durables would spend differently. Similarly, we should expect the national consumption function to be higher after a depression or a war, when people have depleted their stocks of durables, than after a boom, when families are generally well stocked.

One suggested method of explaining purchases of goods is to assume that the stock of durables that people would like to have is related to their income. The actual purchases would then be some portion of the difference between this desired stock and the stock that they already own. This method was used many years ago to predict the sales of automobiles. Unfortunately, it does not lend itself well to statistical study, because of the difficulty of measuring what people would like. A simpler method is to assume that the *purchases* are related to income but that the *level* of purchases is related to the stock of durable goods. (In the usual consumption function, $C = a + bY$, this means that the stock of durable goods affects the size of a; the larger the stock, the smaller is a.)

Thus far we have been considering the effects of the stock of durable goods on the purchases of more durables. The stock of durables also affects consumption of nondurable goods and services.

The possession of most durable goods tends to lessen the need for other consumption. A family with home-laundry equipment has less demand for commercial-laundry services. The total expenditure for food of a family with a home freezer may possibly be decreased. One of the most interesting shifts of this type in recent years has been the substitution of television for commercial entertainment, especially motion pictures. Over a somewhat longer period, private automobiles have substituted for commercial transportation, especially rail travel.

In some respects, however, the possession of certain durable goods may increase consumption of other products which are used jointly with the durable good. This joint-cost element is most important in the case of automobiles, for fuel and maintenance costs usually exceed the cost of the vehicle itself. The increased use of electrically operated durables is an important element in the increased home consumption of electricity. It is probable that, on balance, automobiles increase other consumption whereas other durables decrease consumption.

MONETARY ASSETS

Monetary assets do not render services directly, as do consumer durables. (We will ignore the pleasure the miser receives from contemplating his hoard.) Instead, these assets affect behavior only because they affect the wealth of the consumer and therefore alter his willingness to spend. In this category, we include cash, bank deposits, government and private bonds, personal notes and mortgages, stocks, and, to some extent, jewels and works of art.

In general, one would say that possession of larger monetary assets would increase the willingness of consumers to consume current income. There is no need to save for a rainy day if funds already on hand will take care of a deluge. Thus, we should expect to find some difference in the expenditure patterns of two persons who work side by side if one of them had inherited a substantial sum.

When we step outside the rather narrow confines of inheritance and windfall profits, the case is not so clear. If a family saves for some future goal, we should not expect the successful fulfillment of its program to lessen future efforts. If a program calls for saving $500 each year for 30 years—in order to provide, say, a retirement fund—naturally, the stock of assets will grow. We should not expect this growth to lessen future saving.

But statistics of consumer expenditure indicate that assets do affect saving. At every income level, we observe lower average saving (higher consumption) for those who possess assets than for those who do not. An alternative explanation is that the assets make it easier to dis-save. At every income level, there are some who save and some who dis-save. Those without assets must borrow; those with assets merely use them for consumption and can, if they choose, overspend their income. For this reason, we should expect to find a higher proportion of dis-savers among asset-holders. These dis-savers lower the average saving for the entire group. It is not so clear that asset-holding alters the amount of saving by those who actually save.

In the next chapter, we shall discuss the *Pigou effect*, which is concerned with the effect of price changes upon consumer spending. If the general price level changes, consumers should revalue their assets in terms of the new purchasing power. Some of these assets, especially stocks and other equity investments, will change with the price level, and their purchasing power will consequently be unaffected. Those assets that are measured in purely monetary terms, such as bonds or bank deposits, will remain fixed in dollars. Their purchasing power will therefore fall if prices rise and rise if prices fall.

Assuming that consumers revalue their assets in this fashion, we should expect a fall in the price level to increase the consumption function, since the money assets have increased in value. This reaction plays an important part in analyzing the reaction of the economy to price changes. We shall discuss it in more detail in Chapter 11.

Although we have been discussing only consumer assets, consumer debt is analogous in its effects. One would expect to find that consumers with relatively large debts tend to consume less, for they work to pay off the debts. All the other effects can be similarly analyzed, with consumer debt playing the role of negative consumer assets. Thus, larger debt should have the same effect as smaller assets.

TASTES AND HABITS

The ultimate goal of consumption is to provide satisfaction (or utility) to the consumer. One would therefore imagine that it would be appropriate to include some measure of satisfaction in the consumption function. Unfortunately, no simple measure of taste exists. The usual way of avoiding this dilemma is to assume that consumers' tastes do not change radically from year to year. Such an assumption is more acceptable in our discussion of total consumption than it would be if we were discussing consumption of individual items. All we need assume is that the satisfaction that people derive from consumption now and the satisfaction to be derived from future consumption (saving) change together. As medical progress increases the expected length of life and the years to live on assets, we should expect some change in this preference, but such change takes place slowly. It is therefore ignored in most discussions of the consumption function.

It is sometimes suggested that one should include consumers' *needs*, as opposed to mere taste, in the consumption function. In this sense, one might include some measure of the cost of necessities—food, clothing, and housing. Such a measure is not easily definable, since necessities mean different things to different people. Does "necessary" housing mean a tent, a shack, or a Park Avenue apartment? What kind of clothing is "necessary"? What kind of food? In one recent divorce case, the wife listed the necessary expenses for herself and her child as $3,500 per month. An adequate diet with all essential food elements can be provided for less than half the amount that the average family spends. In view of this wide range of definition, economists have been unable to give any objective meaning to the term *necessity*.

Since tastes tend to harden into habits, several attempts have been made to introduce this habit structure into the consumption function. The simplest way of including it is to use an average of the income of the preceding few years as well as present income. The higher the previous income, the more one would consume *now*, whatever the level of current income. Another way of including past history is to use the highest previous income. Such a formulation assumes that people try to maintain high consumption standards but not low ones.

Although neither of these measures is ideal, either will serve as an index to measure the continuity of consumption patterns.

DISTRIBUTION OF INCOME

If all consumers had exactly the same marginal propensity to consume, the distribution of income would be unimportant. A transfer of income from one man to another would decrease the consumption of one by exactly the amount it increased the consumption of the other. To the extent that the marginal propensity to consume differs from individual to individual, it would be possible to change the total consumption by such transfers. A transfer of $1,000 from a man with a marginal propensity to consume of .50 to a man with a marginal propensity of .75 would increase total consumption by $250.

In the United States, there is some difference between high- and low-income groups in the marginal propensity to consume, but less than most people think. Casual observation tends to concentrate on the *average* propensity to consume, not the *marginal*. A poor man may spend all his income for consumption, but he will not necessarily spend all of any increase he receives. Table 18 lists consumption and income for average families in various income brackets. There is much less variation in the *marginal* propensity to consume than in the *average* propensity to consume. Since our casual impressions are based upon the average propensity, they tend to be misleading. One estimate indicated that if all consumers had the average income, consumption would be 4 percent higher than it is under the present distribution. Moving each consumer halfway to the average would increase consumption by 2½ percent.* These estimates indicate that the possibilities of increasing consumption by redistributing income are quite modest. (Although many left-wing British economists have advocated such a policy, very few American economists have done so.)

TABLE 18

FAMILY INCOME AND CONSUMPTION 1953*

Family Income after Taxes	Consumption Expenditure	Saving
$1,000	$1,100	−$100
2,000	2,050	− 50
3,000	3,000	0
4,000	3,900	100
5,000	4,780	220
6,000	5,650	350
7,000	6,500	500
8,000	7,300	700

* Adapted from projections of the 1950 Bureau of Labor Statistics Survey. For the projections, see "The Consumer Markets, 1954–59," *Fortune* (August 1954).

Even these increases probably overstate the effects of re-distribution. They are computed on the assumption that each individual whose income changed would behave exactly like those who previously had such income. Such an assumption is tenable only if the consumption of each individual is inde-

* See Harold Lubell, "Effects of Redistribution of Income on Consumers' Expenditures," *American Economic Review*, March 1947, 37, 157-170; and his "Correction," *loc. cit.* December 1947, 37, 930.

pendent of that of other individuals. But consumption is not independent, for people try to keep up with the Joneses and ahead of the Smiths. If income were redistributed, those with lower incomes would find that the Joneses are not so hard to keep up with. We should therefore expect somewhat less consumption at each income level than before. Those who are trying to keep ahead of the Smiths will find their task more difficult, since the Smiths may also now have more money. We can therefore say that the "Jones effect" would tend to reduce the gain in consumption caused by redistribution but that the "Smith effect" might tend to raise it. If one can judge by advertisers' concentration on emulation as a motive, it is probable that the "Jones effect" is more important in the United States than elsewhere, although the "Smith effect" may dominate in other countries. On this ground, we may say that redistribution of income, in the United States, at least, is not apt to lead to any great increase in consumption.

CREDIT TERMS

It was once common for economists to include the rate of interest as an important factor in determining consumption and saving—sometimes, indeed, as the only factor. These economists felt that the rate of interest was the price at which one bought future goods by giving up present goods. One would naturally expect that this price would affect the choice between present and future goods, just as any other price affects the amount purchased. But there was some confusion about the direction of this effect. If interest rates were higher, one could gain more by postponing purchase; however, one could obtain the same future goods for less present saving. Whether one would save less or more as rates rose depended upon the relative stability of desires for present goods and future goods. The issue was never really settled.

This debate has now become largely academic in the United States. Years of low interest rates have tended to keep the rate from fluctuating very much. If, as many believe, the incentives toward greater and lesser saving almost cancel each other, then the effects of changes in the rate of interest will be slight. If, in addition, the changes are small, the interest rate can be dropped from the discussion of consumption and saving.

A second factor has also contributed to the decreased importance of the interest rate. In the eighteenth and nineteenth centuries, most saving was done by the richer classes. Many of these people had incomes largely derived from investments. They would naturally be quite sensitive to changes in the interest rate. In modern America, small savers account for a large portion of saving. Even a man with an annual income of $10,000 may save about $1,000 a year. On this sum he can earn, at 4 percent, only $40 annually. This return is less than $\frac{1}{2}$ of 1 percent of his annual income. It is difficult to imagine that he would react very much if the interest rate rose so that he could earn $50 instead of $40.

The increasing importance of durable consumer goods has given credit a new role in the analysis of consumer behavior. Our previous discussion dealt with consumers as lenders;

consumer durables have made them borrowers. Many durables are quite expensive and are therefore often purchased on credit. In some cases, the competition among sellers seems to revolve around liberalized credit terms rather than changed prices. The interest rate itself is seldom important in such calculations; many buyers do not even know the rate on their contracts. The terms of the loan are the important factors, especially the size of the down payment and the period of the loan. During inflationary periods, the United States government caused a substantial decline in sales of such goods with credit regulations. On installment buying, these regulations usually required a 25-percent down payment and payment of the balance within 18 months. Such regulations probably have more effect on buying than any reasonable change in interest rates. Similar effects have also been noted in housing, where the terms are often more important than the interest rate or even the price.

In summary, then, we may say that interest rates have a relatively minor effect on saving and consumption but that credit terms have an important effect on consumption, especially on the purchase of durable goods.

POPULATION

Our previous discussion of consumption by family groups gives us a clue to the role of population in determining consumption. If a family has an income of $6,000, it spends $5,650 on consumption. If the same $6,000 were given to two families, each receiving $3,000, the total consumption would be $6,000, or $3,000 per family. It is therefore clear that the consumption function will be higher if a given income is shared among more people.

A similar effect can be noted from an examination of income and consumption data for families of varying size. Table 19 presents such comparisons. They indicate higher consumption in each income bracket by the larger families. For both these reasons, we say that a larger population means a higher consumption function.

TABLE 19*

CONSUMPTION EXPENDITURES BY INCOME AND FAMILY SIZE 1935–36

Income	Number of Persons in Family		
	2	*3 or 4*	*5 or more*
under $1,000	665	778	817
1,000– 2,000	1178	1280	1294
2,000– 3,000	1832	1943	2092
3,000– 4,000	2546	2566	2676
4,000– 5,000	2281	3186	4037
5,000–10,000	2304	3670	4889

* Summarized from Table 50, U.S. Department of Agriculture, *Family Income and Expenditures, Part 2,* Washington: U.S. Government Printing Office, 1940. These data apply to villages in the middle Atlantic and north central states.

GOVERNMENT AND CONSUMPTION

In the modern world, the government has come to play an increasingly important role in economic life. We noted the influence of the government in the discussion of investment; its influence on consumption is comparable.

The largest single avenue of government influence is its effect on disposable income, which we have previously defined as income minus taxes plus transfer payments. In 1950, transfers amounted to about 5 per cent of income and taxes to about 25 percent. It is clear that changes in either taxes or transfers will affect consumption. In Chapter 4, these effects were analyzed, and multipliers were computed to measure the magnitude of the change. If one wished, the analysis of Chapter 4 could be carried to greater lengths. We have previously noted that different families have different marginal propensities to consume. In particular, this propensity is higher in low income groups and large families, lower in high income groups and small families. A comprehensive study of the effects of tax changes would consider the individuals whose taxes are being changed and would measure the marginal propensity to consume of these taxpayers. Such analysis often underlies political debate on tax changes. We shall not carry our study to such lengths, since these computations are meaningful only in relation to specific tax programs.

The consumption function ordinarily relates consumption to disposable income. The government activities discussed in the foregoing paragraph do not alter the consumption *function*; they change the *amount* of consumption by movement along the function. Other activities of the government change the consumption function itself; that is, they alter the amount that will be consumed at each income level. We have already mentioned the role of credit terms in durable-goods consumption; government regulations can alter these terms. Many of the other regulatory activities of the government also affect consumption. Highway rules affect the demand for certain kinds of automobiles; building codes affect purchases of home furnishings. In a complex society with a widespread program of government activities, the list can be extended almost indefinitely.

Finally, the form of government expenditures bears an important relation to consumption. Many consumer goods have either a competitive or a complementary relationship to government expenditures. New roads might increase the demand for automobiles; a better social-security system may lessen the need for private saving. There are many examples of such relationship, but an estimate of the exact effect would require detailed analysis of the government budget.

The growth of government saving programs may actually increase the total level of consumption in a society. In the typical case, such additional programs are accompanied by increased taxes. One might therefore be inclined to say that such programs merely transfer the saving act from the individual to the government. In some cases, the sum of costs for the government may be less than the sum of the costs for the individuals in the society. We are all aware that one can often buy more retirement income from an insurance company than he could provide by saving the same amount of money. This is possible because many people do not live to collect this sum. All insurance works on this principle. An insurance company can insure a house against fire for a few dollars a year, because most houses do not burn down.

Some things are not insurable. Private companies can offer medical insurance, because only some people get sick every year; they cannot offer unemployment insurance, because too many policy-holders would require payment at the same time. Only the government, with its almost unlimited credit and the power to create money, can offer such insurance. Over the long run, this insurance can be self-supporting, but private companies might find themselves bankrupt in the early years.

For such items, in which the alternatives are private saving or government programs, the government program is apt to be cheaper. An individual must guard against the worst; the government can guard against the average. Because these programs contain an insurance element, their over-all cost may be less. It should be made clear that this saving exists *only* in cases in which private insurance companies cannot supply such coverage. Where coverage is available privately, one must compare the relative efficiency of the government and private companies.

A STATISTICAL CONSUMPTION FUNCTION?

The previous discussions indicate that the analysis of consumption is a very complex matter. It is also one of the areas of economics that lend themselves well to study by teams of specialists. The fields of economics, psychology, and sociology can all add to our understanding of consumption behavior. Since few individual scholars have training in all these fields, the essential work must be done by group study, a relatively slow process. Inevitably, some have sought to short-cut this process by computing statistical consumption functions. This process consists of assuming that the relationship of the past will hold, at least approximately, into the future.

Two different techniques are used for this process, one based upon aggregate income and consumption, the other upon family-budget data. The first is quite simple, at least in principle. It consists of plotting national consumption against national disposable income, as in Figure 21, and drawing a line through these points. The details of such analysis can be

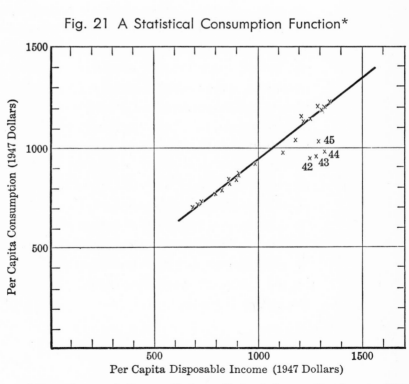

Fig. 21 A Statistical Consumption Function*

* From *Survey of Current Business, National Income Supplement, 1954,* pp. 24–25.

found in any text on statistics. By the use of multiple regression, one can include other variables—for example, population or consumer assets—but the principles are similar. Further refinements are possible, including adjusting national data to a percapita basis and adjusting for prices.

There are two main disadvantages in such analysis. Most of the variables show a relatively steady increase from year to year. It is therefore very difficult to ascribe the proper proportion of change in consumption to the various causal factors.

This continued growth is the source of the other disadvantage. In many cases, the estimate for next year depends upon values of consumption and income which are beyond all previously observed values. In the historic case of this guessing game, many economists attempted, during the latter part of World War II, to predict income and consumption in the postwar period. Since the war years were obviously distorted, such predictions were based on data for 1942 and earlier years. The highest consumption in that period was in 1941—76.6 billion dollars (measured in 1939 dollars). In 1946, consumption was 95.7 billion dollars (still in 1939 dollars). The statisticians were trying to predict a consumption level 25 percent higher than any previously observed. It is not surprising that their efforts were not very successful.

The second method uses consumption patterns as observed among families, then adjusts the total consumption for shifts in the total income. The most famous of these estimates was made by the Consumer Purchases Study. The data used are summarized in Table 20.

TABLE 20

DISTRIBUTION OF CONSUMER INCOMES, 1935-1936*

Percentage Distribution of Consumer Units
with Total Consumer Income of

Income Level	50 Billion Dollars	60 Billion Dollars	70 Billion Dollars	80 Billion Dollars
$ 0–$1,000	56.4	46.2	37.8	31.3
1,000– 2,000	31.5	35.3	36.9	37.0
2,000– 3,000	7.6	11.4	15.1	17.6
3,000– 5,000	2.7	4.7	7.0	9.8
5,000 and over	1.8	2.4	3.2	4.3
	100.0	100.0	100.0	100.0

* National Resources Committee, *Consumer Expenditures in the United States,*
Washington: Government Printing Office, 1939, p. 165.

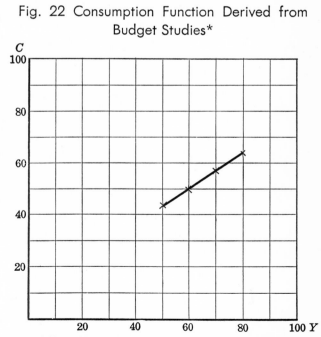

Fig. 22 Consumption Function Derived from
Budget Studies*

* From *National Resources Committee, Consumer Expenditures in the United States,* U.S. Government Printing Office,
1939, p. 167.

In 1935-1936, when the study was made, personal incomes totalled 60 billion dollars. The distribution of that income is indicated in the appropriate column of Table 20. If the same proportionate distribution of income held while total personal income fell to 50 billion dollars, there would be more people in the lowest income group but fewer in all other groups. This distribution is shown in the first column. Table 20 also shows the distribution of income at two higher income levels.

The survey results indicate the total consumption of families in each bracket. If we multiply the consumption pattern in each bracket by the percentage in that bracket and add all the figures so obtained, we can obtain a total consumption function. Figure 22 shows the consumption function derived from this process.

This process has not been notably more successful than estimation based on aggregate data. Considering the previous discussion of habits and relations of consumers, we would not expect consumers whose incomes move up proportionately to behave exactly like those who previously had that income. Indeed, later studies seem to indicate that, if all consumers move up together, each tends to save the same percentage of his income as *he* previously saved. This result is not sufficiently certain to permit prediction either, so this whole method has been substantially abandoned.

The rather dismal conclusion to which we must come is that there is no substitute for full study of the consumption process. Statistics can be tremendously helpful in this study, for verifying hypotheses and suggesting new ones, but they will not replace full study.

DISCUSSION QUESTIONS

1. If the purchase of consumer durables were treated as saving and depreciation on these durables as consumption, would you expect more or less change in consumption from year to year? Would you expect the consumption function to be steeper or flatter?

2. Much saving is now contractual—*e.g.*, in insurance policies. What effect does this have on the consumption function?

3. Habits of consumption have been introduced into the consumption function. Do you think saving habits might also be important? Which would matter more if incomes fell? if they rose?

4. What effect has the growth of hospitalization insurance on the need for savings? on the consumption function?

5. (*For students with a background in statistics*) Enumerate some of the problems to be faced in estimating a consumption function by statistical techniques.

SUGGESTED ADDITIONAL READINGS

There are very few general works on consumption and saving relations, but articles on specific studies or aspects abound.

Of the books, one must mention James S. Duesenberry, *Income, Saving, and the Theory of Consumer Behavior* (Cambridge, Mass.: Harvard University Press, 1949). This volume introduced explicitly the social aspects of consumption and indicated also the role of previous income in determining current consumption. George Katona, *Psychological Aspects of Economic Behavior* (New York: McGraw-Hill, 1951), describes some aspects of the study of consumer behavior by survey techniques. The symposium *Savings in the Modern Economy*, edited by Heller, Boddy, and Nelson (Minneapolis: University of Minnesota Press, 1953), discusses many aspects of saving and consumption behavior. Especially interesting is Chapter 13, by Duesenberry, Dorothy Brady, Imrie de Vegh, James Morgan, Margaret G. Reid, James Tobin, David McCord Wright, and Simon Kuznets.

An indication of the variety of the statistical studies that have been made can be found in the following articles in the *Review of Economic Statistics:* Bassie, August 1946; George Katona and Rensis Likert, Louis H. Bean, Irwin Friend, E. G. Bennion, and Dorothy S. Brady, November 1946; Everett Hagen, May 1947; W. S. Woytinsky, February 1948; and Nathan Koffsky, February 1948.

On the role of asset holdings, see James Tobin, "Asset Holdings and Spending Decisions," American Economic Review, *Papers and Proceedings, 42*:2 (May 1952).

On the effects of income redistribution, see the article by Lubell referred to in the text (p. 157).

CHAPTER 11

Aggregate Demand

IN THE PREVIOUS CHAPTERS, we have discussed the various factors that alter the demand for goods and services. We have considered at some length the decisions of investors and consumers and we have examined the effects of government decisions. We have also examined the money market and its effects upon these demand decisions. Each change in these factors has been analyzed in terms of its effect on the amount of goods and services that would be purchased. We must now consider the effects of price changes. In preceding chapters, we have been examining elements that shift the demand curve; we now want to see what shape the demand curve has as we move along it to a different price. This order is the opposite of that usually followed in discussing the demand for a specific product; the price usually is considered first, then the factors that shift the curve. There are two reasons for the present reversal of order. The first is simplicity: the analysis of price changes involves many of the elements that we have previously discussed. It is therefore easier to discuss price changes now, after we have discussed the other details of aggregate demand.

The second reason is institutional. In a society like that of the United States, there are substantial elements of monopoly. These are evident both in product markets and in labor markets. Where such elements exist, prices tend to have a certain rigidity and often change in jumps rather than smoothly. It is therefore a reasonably satisfactory approximation to say that the aggregate supply curve is flat up to the full-employment output. Beyond full employment, some slight increases in output may be possible, but increases in demand provide mainly increases in price. Such a supply curve is shown in Figure 23.

If the aggregate supply curve is flat, there tend to be relatively few changes in price. The national income is determined at the level at which the aggregate demand curve crosses this supply curve. Since shifts in the demand curve do not usually result in price changes, it is more useful to concentrate on those factors that cause shifts in the demand schedule than to discuss the effects of movements along the demand curve.

Supply and demand curves for individual products are measured in terms of price and quantity. For society as a whole, we can use the price level to measure the price, but we have no corresponding physical measurement for the quantity. In place of such a measure, we usually use national product, adjusted to eliminate the effects of price changes. Since national product and national income are the same, we can represent this quantity by Y^*. (As indicated in Chapter 2, we represent this adjustment for prices by adding an asterisk to the usual symbol.)

THE KEYNES EFFECT

The question of the effect of price changes upon aggregate demand has an important place in discussions of anti-depression policy. Many businessmen and some economists argue that a depression can be cured if only workers will agree to accept reduced wages. Lower wages, they claim, would lower business costs and induce greater output. This would certainly be true of any single firm or industry whose workers would accept lower wages; it should therefore be true of the whole society.

Other economists argue that this view is a delusion. If the workers of one firm accept reduced wages, there will be little or no change in the demand of that firm, since most of the

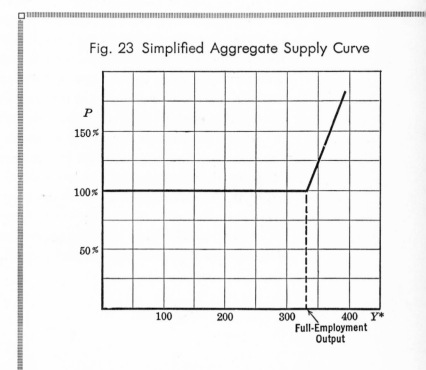

Fig. 23 Simplified Aggregate Supply Curve

customers are not employees. But if all firms cut wages, the demand will fall, since the employees of one firm are the customers of others. The net effect would be merely a lower wage level and price level, but no change in the total amount of sales. (It is true that there might be some flurry of increased output after wages fell and before prices fell, but the increase would be only temporary.)

Keynes, in his *General Theory*, discussed this problem. In effect, he considered each of the functions involved in determining aggregate demand to see if price had any effect. Let us follow his reasoning.

The marginal efficiency of capital is based upon the relative size of present costs and future returns. If prices fall and are expected to stay at the new level, then future returns fall in exactly the same degree as present purchase prices. If there is no change in interest rates, the investments that were previously profitable are still profitable, and those that were unprofitable are still unprofitable. So long as we adjust the dollar value of investment for price changes, there will be no change in the marginal efficiency of capital. (In terms of the graphic analysis that we have used, we need only add an asterisk to I.)

If the government is buying a certain set of goods and services, then government expenditures rise with prices. If Congress votes a pay increase, it must vote a corresponding increase in the budget. (Here again we need only add the asterisk.)

Keynes's discussion of the consumption function follows along similar lines. He believed that consumers made their decisions on the basis of purchasing power. Thus, if incomes and prices fall uniformly, there is no reason to assume that consumers will change their actual purchases, although the dollar value of these purchases would fall. (Again, merely adding asterisks to indicate adjustment for price-level changes would be sufficient.)

Since these three relationships constitute the description of the commodity market, Keynes concluded that there would be no change in the commodity equilibrium curve as a result of changes in the price level.

Examining the demand for money, we should expect to find the same phenomenon. If all prices are lower, less money will be needed to finance day-to-day transactions. Similarly, one should expect investors' liquidity preference to be stated in terms of purchasing power. Thus, the demand for money remains unchanged after adjustment for price changes.

There remains only the supply of money. Here, however, we notice a change as the price level changes. As prices fall, incomes and consumption may fall, but a dollar bill remains a dollar bill. If the money supply is 110 billion dollars and the price level falls to half its former level, the purchasing power of the money supply becomes 220 billion dollars. We would therefore expect a lower price to have the same effect as an increase in the money supply.

An increase in the money supply has the effect of shifting the money equilibrium curve to the right. Thus, a lower price should have the same effect. As the money equilibrium curve shifts, the interest rate will fall and income will increase. These effects are shown in Figure 24.

As this illustration indicates, when the price falls from P_1 to P_2, the interest rate falls from 10 to 2 percent and income increases to about 350 billion dollars. However, as price falls below P_2, the only changes that would take place in the money equilibrium curve are beyond the intersection with the commodity equilibrium curve. This is so because in these graphs 2 percent is the minimal interest rate. In Chapter 7, we observed that, at some low interest rate, security holders would be willing to hold any amount of money rather than to bid down interest rates any further. In Figure 24, 2 percent is that bottom rate.

TABLE 21

THE KEYNES EFFECT

(Unit: one billion dollars)

Part A: Transactions Demand for Money		Part B: Money Demand Equals Money Supply†				Part C: Liquidity Preference	
		$P=100$		$P=65$			
Y^*	M_1^*	M_1^*	M_2^*	M_1^*	M_2^*	r	M_2^*
50	24	0	110	0	170	12%	5
100	45	10	100	30	140	10	11
150	63	30	80	60	110	8	20
200	78	50	60	90	80	6	32
250	90	70	40	120	50	4	47
300	99	90	20	150	20	2	65
350	105	110	0	170	0		or more
400	108						

† Assuming that $M_s=110$. When $P=100$, $M_s^*=110$; when $P=65$, $M_s^*=170$.

Table 21 shows the derivation of the money equilibrium curve for two price levels. The basic data for the transactions demand for money and liquidity preference are the same as those of Table 14 (p. 105).

If we derive a money equilibrium curve using the $P=100$ column of Table 21, we obtain the same result as in Chapter 7. For example, at an income of 250 billion dollars, 90 billion dollars are required for M_1^*. This leaves 20 billion dollars to

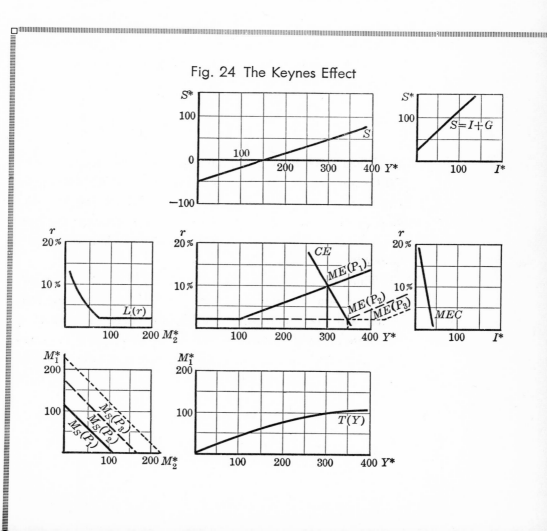

Fig. 24 The Keynes Effect

satisfy liquidity preference and forces interest rates to 8 percent. The complete schedule is given in Table 22.

TABLE 22

MONEY EQUILIBRIUM CURVES
(Unit: one billion dollars)

$P=100$		$P=65$	
Y^*	r	Y^*	r
50	2%	50	2%
100	2	100	2
150	4	150	2
200	6	200	2
250	8	250	2
300	10	300	2
350	12	350	2
		400	3

When price falls to 65, the effective money supply rises to 170 billion dollars. At all income levels below 350 billion dollars, there is still more than 65 billion dollars left to satisfy liquidity preference. Thus, the interest rate remains at the 2-percent minimum. This money equilibrium curve is also shown in Table 22.

Thus, we have seen that a decline in prices tends to force the money equilibrium curve to the right. This moves the intersection with the commodity equilibrium curve to a lower interest rate and higher income, unless the interest rate is already at the minimal level, in which case price changes have no further effect.

The aggregate demand curve which results from this analysis is shown in Figure 25. The real income demanded never exceeds the level shown by the commodity equilibrium curve at the minimal rate of interest. In our example, this level is about 350 billion dollars.

Following this line of reasoning, Keynes argued that there were limits beyond which demand would not increase, however low the price. It was entirely possible that this limit might not be enough to provide jobs for all who were willing to work. If the unemployed tried to obtain work by bidding down wages, other people might become unemployed, but total employment would not change. He therefore proposed that depressions be fought by increasing government spending, to shift the aggregate demand curve, rather than by placing our faith in expansion through lowered prices.

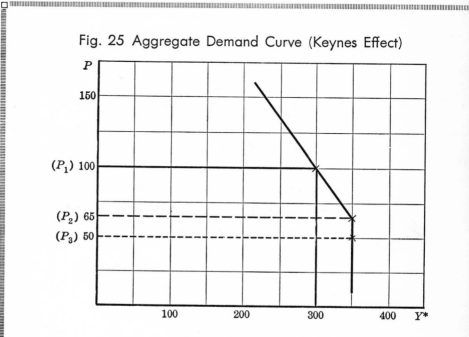

Fig. 25 Aggregate Demand Curve (Keynes Effect)

THE PIGOU EFFECT

Keynes's conclusions were unacceptable to two groups. The first group objected because his analysis made government intervention or continued depression the only two possible alternatives. Many members of this group opposed government intervention on principle and therefore rejected this choice as undesirable.

The second group opposed Keynes's conclusions on logical rather than political grounds. To them, it seemed impossible that workers could not find jobs by cutting their wages sufficiently. Among this group was A. C. Pigou, who discussed the question in his article "The Classical Stationary State." He observed that price changes would alter the consumption function. This reaction has come to be known as the *Pigou effect.*

In Chapter 10, we mentioned the role of consumer assets as determinants of consumption. An increase in consumer assets tends to increase the willingness of consumers to spend their current income for consumption. A decline in prices tends to raise the value of money assets and therefore to raise the consumption function.

Let us consider in detail the effects upon consumers of a change in prices. As prices fall, incomes tend to fall proportionately. Thus, a consumer with no assets would find himself in the same position as before the decline in prices. Even if he has durable consumer assets, they decline in money value with price. The same is usually true of stocks. Only bonds and cash tend to maintain their money value, which means a rise in purchasing power. This increase in purchasing power tends to raise consumption and lower saving.

Imagine a very simplified example. We suppose that an individual has a disposable income of $5,000 per year and expects to work for 30 years. He would like to have a retirement fund equal to six years' income. Accordingly, each year he spends $4,000 for consumption and saves $1,000. By the end of 10 years, he has saved $10,000. Now suppose that prices, and his income, are cut in half. He now earns $2,500 and can buy the same consumption goods as before for $2,000. But what about his saving needs? His retirement goal of six years' income is now $15,000. Since he has 20 years to go, he can reach the goal by saving $250 each year. Thus, he can maintain his old consumption level and achieve his old saving goal for $2,250— less than his income. He will probably spend at least a part of the extra $250 on consumption, thus raising his standard of living and his consumption function. This increase in consumption is possible because the fall in price has put him 10 years ahead on his saving program.

The rise in the consumption function associated with a lower price level means a lower saving function. The fall in the saving function moves the commodity equilibrium curve to the right, tending to increase the rate of interest and the level of income. Such a shift is shown in Figure 26.

Since there are no flat portions of the commodity equilibrium curve, there is no limit to the amount of expansion of aggregate demand that can come about through the Pigou effect.

The aggregate demand curve has the shape indicated in Figure 27.

This result satisfied Pigou. He had proved that it was always possible to obtain full employment if wages and prices fell sufficiently. As a logical proposition, this conclusion was almost indisputable, and Pigou claimed nothing more than logic. Strangely enough, this result also satisfied the political opponents of Keynes, who could now blame unemployment on the unwillingness of workers to accept lower wages, for Pigou

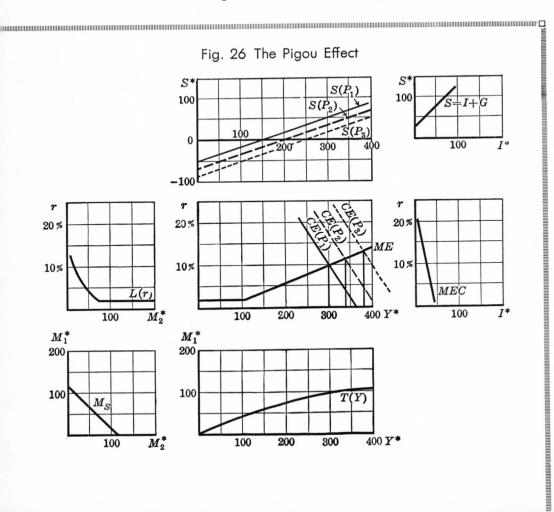

Fig. 26 The Pigou Effect

had shown that there exists *some* level of wages that would be compatible with full employment. If the Pigou effect was to have important practical effects, it was also necessary to show that the full-employment wage level was not too far from the present level. If the equilibrium wage were very different from the present level, it might be compatible with full employment if attained, but the process of reaching it might be hopelessly disruptive. (Imagine the difficulties if full employment could be attained only at an average wage of 10 cents an hour.)

The question of how much wages should average could not be answered by any purely theoretical analysis. Only statistical study, concerned with the size of consumer assets and the effects of assets upon consumption, could offer even a tentative hypothesis. The present data are inadequate for decision. Those who believe in the Pigou effect find statistical "proof"; unbelievers find statistical "disproof." This controversy is a con-

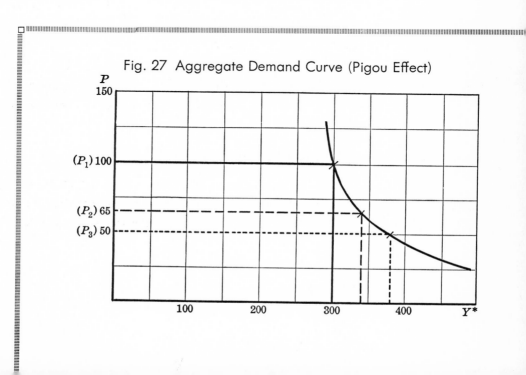

Fig. 27 Aggregate Demand Curve (Pigou Effect)

tinuing one; for the present status of the debate, the reader must consult current journal articles.

THE AGGREGATE DEMAND CURVE

To obtain an aggregate demand curve, we must combine the Pigou effect and the Keynes effect. Suppose we choose a price at random. For this price there is a corresponding specific effective money supply and a specific consumption function. Using these functions, we can draw the appropriate commodity equilibrium curve and money equilibrium curve. Their intersection gives the corresponding income. If we repeat this process for other prices, we obtain other incomes. Connecting these gives us the aggregate demand curve. Such a process is shown in Figure 28.

Figure 28 shows that decreases in price cause an increase in aggregate demand—that is, in national income. It is impossible to foretell the net effect of the price change on the interest rate. The Keynes effect tends to lower the interest rate; the Pigou effect tends to raise the interest rate. The net result of both might be in the direction of either higher or lower interest rates, depending upon the relative size of the two effects.

PRICES CHANGED AND CHANGING

The analysis of this chapter deals with the level of aggregate demand at various price levels. We found that lower prices mean higher aggregate demand. In dealing with aggregate de-

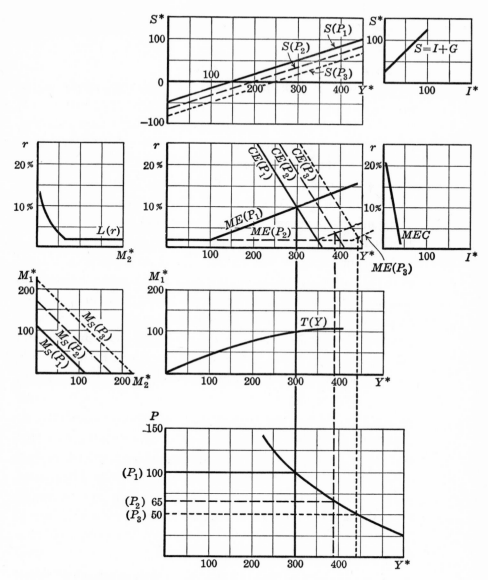

Fig. 28 Derivation of Aggregate Demand Curve

mand as well as with the demand for individual products, we must distinguish this effect from the analysis of falling prices. If prices are falling and people expect them to fall even further, consumers and investors may postpone their purchases until prices reach the lowest level. This is especially true of the purchases of durable and semidurable goods which can be postponed. Similarly, although *higher* prices discourage spending, *rising* prices encourage it if they create the expectation of further increases.

The problem of expectation affects all aspects of the analysis of aggregate demand. If prices fall but are expected to rise later, investment may be encouraged, since present costs decline but future revenue does not. In such circumstances, however, the Pigou effect would not operate, for individuals would not revalue their assets. If one expects to spend his assets only after retirement, he will revalue them only if he expects prices in the future to be different. A temporary fall in price will therefore cause no revaluation of assets and, consequently, no change in consumption. In some cases, a temporary fall might even cause a decrease in consumption. Some forms of saving, especially through insurance or payroll-deduction plans, tend to be fixed in dollars. A decline in prices and income would leave these programs unaffected; therefore, less money would be available for consumption. If the price decline were permanent, these programs would probably be rewritten, but a temporary decline would not induce such revision. Thus, a temporary fall might tend to decrease consumption although a permanent fall would increase it.

For all these reasons, one must be very careful in using this analysis to describe dynamic processes. It is intended to describe only the effects of different levels of price, not the movements between them.

DISCUSSION QUESTIONS

1. Is the Pigou effect apt to be more or less important now than in the past? Why?

2. From your own observation, estimate the size of the Pigou effect. Does this estimate give you much faith in its efficacy in preventing depression?

3. From a current *Federal Reserve Bulletin*, find the rate of interest on the most recent issue of long-term governmental securities. What do you conclude from this about the strength of the Keynes effect?

4. On the basis of your answer to question 3, what is the shape of the aggregate demand curve?

SUGGESTED ADDITIONAL READINGS

The Keynes effect is set forth in J. M. Keynes, *The General Theory of Employment, Interest and Money* (New York: Harcourt Brace, 1936), Chapter 19. The Pigou effect is described in A. C. Pigou, "The Classical Stationary State," *Economic Journal*, December 1943, and in "Economic Progress in a Stable Environment," *Economica*, August 1947, reprinted in Lloyd C. Mints (ed.), *Readings in Monetary Theory* (New York: Blakiston, 1951). See also Keynes's *General Theory*, paragraph 3, pages 92-93, for a possible forerunner of Pigou.

On the general subject of price flexibility and aggregate

demand, see James Tobin, "Money Wage Rates and Employment," in Seymour Harris, *The New Economics* (New York: Knopf, 1950), or "Asset Holdings and Spending Decisions," *American Economic Review, Papers and Proceedings, 42:2* (May 1952). This subject was also explored by Don Patinkin, "Price Flexibility and Full Employment," *American Economic Review, 38:4* (September 1948), reprinted in *Readings in Monetary Theory.*

CHAPTER 12

Aggregate Supply

I N THE ANALYSIS of national income, economists have given most of their attention to the determinants of aggregate demand, with relatively little attention to the conditions of supply. In Chapter 11 we mentioned one possible reason for this neglect: A case can be made for believing that the aggregate supply curve is generally horizontal until full employment is reached and almost vertical thereafter. The primary reason for neglecting the aggregate supply curve is quite different: Since the aggregate is believed to be almost exactly the same as the supply curve of an individual product, there is no need of especial elaboration.

In order to understand the conditions of supply, let us briefly review the analysis of the behavior of a single firm. The objective of the firm is to make as much profit as possible. We will assume that the firm is purely competitive, so that it is faced with a given price and a given wage over which it has no control. In order to maximize its profits, the firm must adjust its level of production—the only variable within its control. Since we are considering only short-run analysis, the firm's output will depend only upon the inputs of the variable factors of production, especially labor. Capital equipment and other fixed factors of production are not variable in the short run.

We imagine that this firm has a schedule by which it knows the amount of output it can obtain from any given input of labor. In order to tell whether to hire an additional worker, it must compare the value of the added (or marginal) product with the added cost of hiring the worker. This is merely another way of stating the principle that firms adjust their production until marginal cost equals marginal revenue. The marginal cost of an additional worker is his wage; the marginal revenue is his marginal product times the price.

This same result can be obtained in another way. If a worker can produce 100 units of output per week and his wage is only 80 times the price of the unit of output, hiring him yields a profit of 20 units of output. Firms will continue to expand until the marginal output of the last worker is only as high as the number of units of output that his wage will buy.

As we widen our horizon from a single firm to an entire industry, the same principles apply. The only difference is that more workers are employed and more output is produced, but the same ratios among wages, prices, and marginal product apply.

When we pass from an industry to the nation, we still use the same principles but must apply special techniques of measurement. We can no longer measure output by means of simple quantity or simple price. We must measure national output in terms of real national income and price by using a price index. (Although we speak of *the* wage rate, this rate is merely an average of all rates and is used as an index of labor costs.)

Let us then list the variables and relationships that are required to determine the aggregate supply curve. (As we have done before, we are using general functions when we do not have enough information to give an exact relationship.)

VARIABLES:

Endogenous

$Y^* =$ Real income = national product.

N = Employment.

$\dfrac{\Delta Y^*}{\Delta N} =$ Marginal product.

$w^* =$ Real wage.

Exogenous

P = General price level.

w = Money wage rate.

EQUATIONS:

(1) $w^* = \dfrac{w}{P}.$

(2) $w^* = \dfrac{\Delta Y^*}{\Delta N}.$

(3) $Y^* = F(N).$ (Production function)

(4) $\dfrac{\Delta Y^*}{\Delta N} = F'(N)$.   (Marginal productivity)

(5) $w = w_0$.

These equations restate the principles given above for profit maximization. Equation 3 tells us that the national product depends upon the number of people employed. The marginal product (which is the increase in real income per additional worker) can be derived from the production function. Equation 4 records this relationship, using $F'(N)$ to indicate the marginal-productivity function, which is derived from the total product function, $F(N)$, given in equation 3. Equation 1 defines the real wage as the money wage divided by the price level. Equation 2 is the condition for profit maximization: marginal product must equal the real cost of hiring the worker, the real wage. Finally, equation 5 indicates that the money wage is a factor beyond the scope of the present discussion. Some of the problems of its determination will be discussed in the next chapter. Since there are six variables here and only five equations, we cannot solve for values of the variables. All we can do is draw up an aggregate supply schedule, to be combined with the aggregate demand curve of Chapter 11.

The derivation of such a supply curve is shown in Table 23. Part A corresponds to equation 1; Part B, to equation 4; and Part C, to equation 3. Part B is derived from Part C. For each employment level, we measure the increase in output that accompanied the last increase in employment and divide to obtain

TABLE 23

DERIVATION OF AN AGGREGATE SUPPLY CURVE

Part A: The Real Wage†		Part B: Marginal Productivity		Part C: Production Function	
P (%)	w*	N (in millions)	$\frac{\Delta Y^*}{\Delta N}$	N (in millions)	Y* (in billions)
60	$8,333	10	$7,000	10	$ 70
70	7,143	20	6,500	20	135
80	6,250	30	6,000	30	195
90	5,555	40	5,500	40	250
100	5,000	50	5,000	50	300
110	4,545	60	4,500	60	345

† Assuming a money wage of $5,000.

the marginal product per worker. In the simplified example given here, these increases are measured in units of 10 million men, but they would ordinarily be measured in much smaller units.

In order to derive an aggregate supply curve, we begin with a price level chosen at random—say, 100 percent. At that level, a money wage of $5,000 means $5,000 in purchasing power (Part A). Since the profit maximizing rule of equation 2 says that the real wage should equal the marginal product, we search for a marginal product of $5,000. We find such productivity at an employment of 50 million men (Part B). The production function (Part C) tells us that 50 million men can produce 300 billion dollars of output, measured at base-year prices. Thus, we have found that at a price level of 100 percent total product supplied will be worth 300 billion dollars. Using other prices, we can find other points on the supply curve. (In order to find exact points, it would be necessary to add some intermediate values to one or more parts of Table 23.) Such a supply curve might properly be considered Part *D* of Table 23.

TABLE 24

HYPOTHETICAL AGGREGATE SUPPLY CURVE†

$P(\%)$	Y^* (in billions)
71	70
77	135
83	195
91	250
100	300
111	345

† Assuming a money wage of $5,000.

The same analysis is shown in graphic form in Figure 29. Each part of the figure corresponds to a part of Table 23. Starting with a price chosen at random, we find the corresponding real wage in Part *A*. In Part *B* we find the level of employment for which the marginal product is equal to that wage. Part *C* gives the national product corresponding to that level of employment. This product is plotted in Part *D* opposite the starting price. Repeating the process gives the aggregate supply curve. Note that the axes of the aggregate supply curve are reversed from those of the aggregate demand curve of Chapter 11.

It would be well to pause at this point to remind ourselves of the assumptions that underlie this analysis. We have assumed that the level of employment depends only upon the desires of employers—that is, that the labor supply always exceeds the demand for labor. Such is usually the case at less than full employment.

More important is the assumption of pure competition.

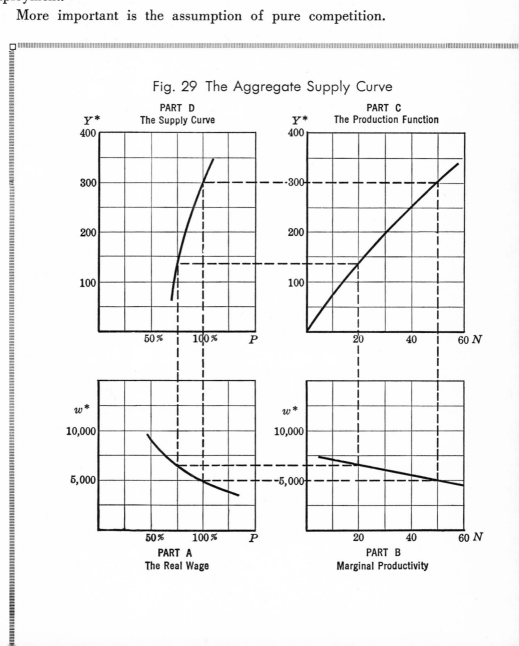

Fig. 29 The Aggregate Supply Curve

PART D
The Supply Curve

PART C
The Production Function

PART A
The Real Wage

PART B
Marginal Productivity

Some economists have argued that our economy is almost purely competitive. They find the differences between the actual results and those of a purely competitive society negligible. If this analysis is correct, the assumption yields the correct results. For the skeptical (including the author), the analysis of this chapter should be regarded merely as a preliminary step to the more advanced discussion presented in Chapter 13.

PROBLEMS

1. The production function is as follows:

N	Y^*
10	$ 75
20	145
30	210
40	270
50	325
60	375

The money wage is $6,000 per year. Find the aggregate supply curve.

2. What is the equilibrium level of income and prices if the aggregate demand is:

P	Y^*
120%	$300
110	325
100	350
90	375
80	400

SUGGESTED ADDITIONAL READINGS

The analysis of this chapter is merely an extension of the theory of the firm in pure competition which can be found in any principles textbook. More precisely, it is adapted from O. H. Brownlee, "Money, Price Level, and Employment," in Francis M. Boddy (ed.), *Applied Economic Analysis*, (New York: Pitman, 1948).

CHAPTER 13

Market Imperfections and Aggregate Supply

IN THE PRECEDING CHAPTER, we discussed the general description of an aggregate supply curve on the assumption of pure competition and adequate labor supply. In part, these assumptions are contradictory, for pure competition in the labor market would cause the real wage to fall to a level at which all available workers would be employed. We must therefore adjust our picture of aggregate supply to account for the conditions of labor supply. If we wish to make our picture more representative of the real world, we must also consider the effects of certain taxes and of monopoly and other restrictions on the product market.

LABOR SUPPLY

In Chapter 12 we considered the shape of the aggregate supply curve as determined by the decisions of employers. We discussed the problems of profitability and found that employ-ment demand depends upon marginal productivity. We may then refer to the marginal product curve as the demand curve for labor.

The supply curve of labor depends upon quite different factors. In the simplest form, workers supply their labor if the marginal utility of income exceeds the marginal disutility of labor. The marginal utility of income is compounded of the marginal utility per dollar and the dollars per hour of work. As wage rates rise, the former declines and the latter rises. It is therefore possible that a rise in wage rates will cause either an increase or a decrease in the amount of labor supplied. For the sake of simplicity, we will assume that increased real wages always lead to increased labor supply.

Let us now examine the shape of the aggregate supply curve, assuming that it depends only upon the preferences of employees. If the money wage rate is fixed, real wages will vary inversely with the price level. The higher the price level, the lower will be the real wage, and the fewer workers will be available. Since fewer workers cannot produce large outputs, we are led to the conclusion that total production would be less at high prices, greater at low prices. The aggregate supply curve based upon workers' decisions is shown in Figure 30, to-gether with its derivation from the labor supply curve. This figure is the same as Figure 29, except that it depends upon the supply of labor (workers' decisions) instead of the demand for labor (employers' decisions).

We now have two aggregate supply curves, one based upon

demand for labor, the other upon supply of labor. These two supply curves are shown in Figure 31. If the price were always at 100%, it would make no difference which curve we chose. For all other prices, we must take whichever curve is less. Employment requires agreement of employer and employee, so each holds a veto power. Employment can never exceed the amount

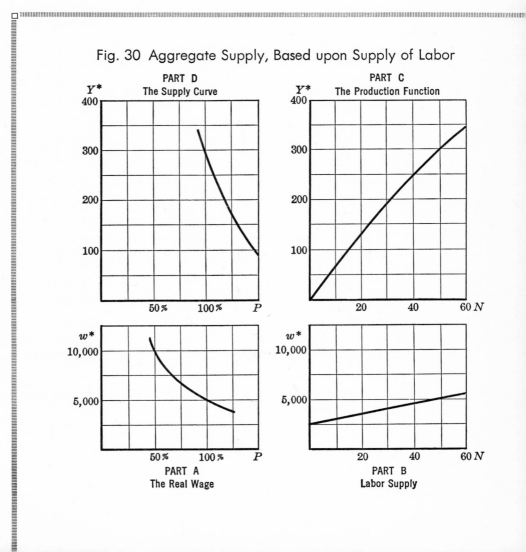

Fig. 30 Aggregate Supply, Based upon Supply of Labor

indicated by either the supply of labor (N_s) or the demand for labor (N_D). Thus the aggregate supply curve is actually bending backward above 100%.

Figures 30 and 31 clearly show that there is some level of employment which cannot be exceeded, whatever the real wage. This level of employment is determined by the intersection of

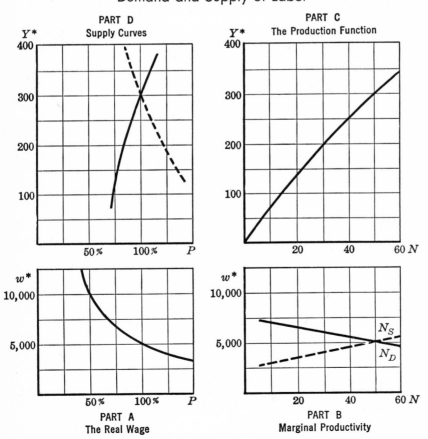

Fig. 31 Aggregate Supply Curves, Based upon
Demand and Supply of Labor

the labor supply and demand curves and is 50 million. It may properly be called full employment, for all who are willing to work are working. Similarly, 100 percent is the price which will bring about full employment.

All this analysis assumes a fixed level of money wages. In such a case, as prices fall and real wages rise, the supply of labor exceeds the demand for labor. We therefore find unemployment at low prices. At the other end of the scale, when prices rise and real wages fall, the demand for labor exceeds the supply. At high prices, we therefore find unfilled jobs. In these circumstances, how realistic is the assumption of fixed money wages?

Any question of empirical relevance is difficult to answer with certainty. Many people would feel that the assumption is half correct in that workers are often willing to accept unemployment rather than a cut in money wages. In the other direction, employers are not so apt to resist wage increases when prices are high. Thus, one might expect money wages to increase proportionately with prices above 100 percent. The most realistic aggregate supply curve might therefore be of the shape shown in Figure 32. This supply curve is determined by the demand for labor up to full employment. It then becomes vertical as firms raise wages to match price changes.

The argument we have given here indicates that there is a long-run pressure in favor of higher wages. If workers resist wage cuts, even at the cost of unemployment, wages will remain steady in bad times. If employers would rather pay higher wages than have unfilled jobs, wages will rise in good times. We shall discuss long-run wage policy later, but we can see now that wages, left to themselves, have a tendency to upward bias.

EXCISE TAXES AND SUPPLY

Excise or sales taxes have the same effect on the aggregate supply curve as on the supply curve of an individual product. The tax creates a difference between the price paid by customers and the amount received by producers. In order to determine the quantity of goods that will be supplied at a given price, it is necessary to subtract the sales tax to find the producers' receipts. Then the analysis follows the lines given above. Figure 33 demonstrates the adjustment for taxes; the lower supply curve

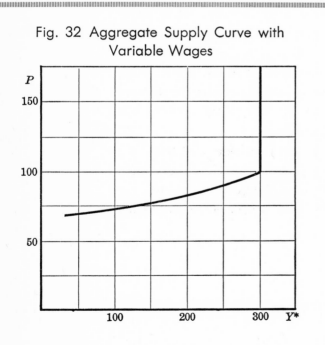

Fig. 32 Aggregate Supply Curve with Variable Wages

indicates supply without tax, and the upper curve indicates the
supply with imposition of the tax.

In practice, the analysis is not quite so simple, since many
of our taxes are not imposed uniformly on all products. Many
state sales taxes exempt certain kinds of products. The federal
excise-tax structure is a collection of varying rates established
according to revenue needs, characteristics of particular industries, and equity considerations. At any given level of national income, the distribution of purchases among the various
industries will be approximately given. Thus the amount of
excise tax can be estimated approximately for every level of
national income. From these estimates, it is possible to construct
a relation between an aggregate supply curve including excise
taxes and the aggregate supply excluding taxes.

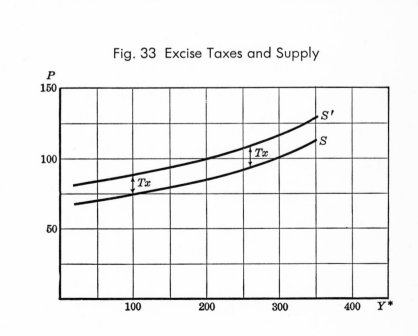

Fig. 33 Excise Taxes and Supply

MONOPOLY

In our society, there are a number of elements of monopoly and monopolistic practice. In analyzing pure competition, we can confine our attention to price; in monopoly, the marginal revenue differs from price. It is often said, in this sense, that a monopolist has no supply curve, for the amount he will sell depends upon the shape of the demand curve as well as upon the price.

It is possible to construct an aggregate supply curve even though we cannot construct individual supply curves. In order to do this, we use the same kind of reasoning that we used for excise taxes. For every level of national income, there is a specific distribution of the product among various industries. For each industry that is monopolized, there exists some ratio between marginal revenue and price. (For competitive indus-

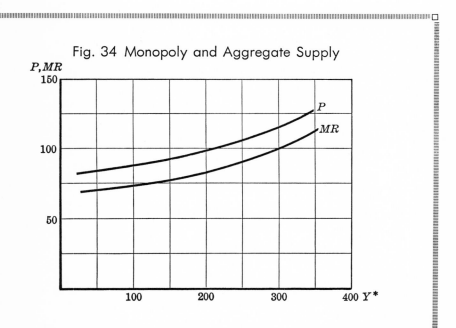

Fig. 34 Monopoly and Aggregate Supply

tries, the ratio is one, for price and marginal revenue are the same.) By taking a weighted average of these ratios, we can obtain a ratio between marginal revenue and price for the entire society at every income level. The supply depends upon the marginal revenue, but purchases depend upon the price. Figure 34 shows the relationship between these two curves. The curve labeled *MR* is the same as the supply curve previously derived; the curve labeled *P* is obtained simply by increasing the level of the *MR* curve by the ratio of price to marginal revenue. An increase in the degree of monopoly will widen the gap.

For those who prefer to think of it in this fashion, the presence of the monopoly has the same effect on the supply curve as the imposition of a sales tax. In this case, however, the tax is imposed by the monopolist, not the government. An increase in the degree of monopoly is the same as an increase in the tax.

DISCUSSION QUESTIONS

1. If all labor had "escalator clauses" making money wages directly responsive to the cost of living, what would the effect be on aggregate supply? Would you consider this effect good?

2. How realistic do you consider the assumptions made in the text about wage policy of employers and workers? If you were to alter these assumptions, what would be the resultant supply curve?

3. If excise taxes were levied most heavily on luxuries, how would the supply curve be affected?

CHAPTER 14

Supply and Demand

To FIND the final equilibrium of supply and demand, we need merely set down the results of previous chapters. If we take the aggregate demand curve of Chapter 11 and the aggregate supply curve of Chapters 12 or 13, we can find the final equilibrium values of the price level and of real national income. Such a process is shown in Figure 35.

We should pause here to summarize those variables which are included in this system but which have not been explained. In the demand system are the three government fiscal variables —government expenditures, transfers, and taxes—the money supply, and assets in the hands of consumers. This last variable is essentially the result of history—particularly, of the saving history of consumers. In the supply system, the principal unexplained variable is the money wage rate. Changes in any of these variables would change the equilibrium level of prices and of income. If we had enough information about all the relevant functions, the direction and magnitude of the change could be computed from the system given here.

In addition to these omitted variables, of course, any change in one of the component functions (consumption function, etc.) will change these equilibrium values.

The relation of all the component functions to these summary supply and demand curves is shown in Figure 36. This figure is a summary diagram, covering the general outlines of the analysis given previously. The demand portions repeat Figure 28 (p. 185); the supply portions repeat Figure 29 (p. 195). The appropriate adjustments to account for increased government spending or to allow for the influence of labor market conditions could be made by use of other figures as the models for the parts of this one. All the analysis of this book can be summarized in this one graph.

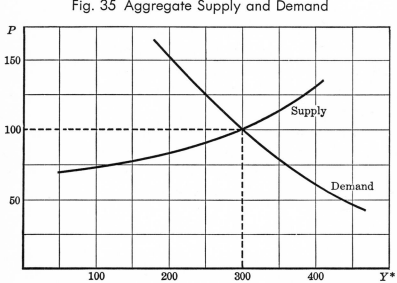

Fig. 35 Aggregate Supply and Demand

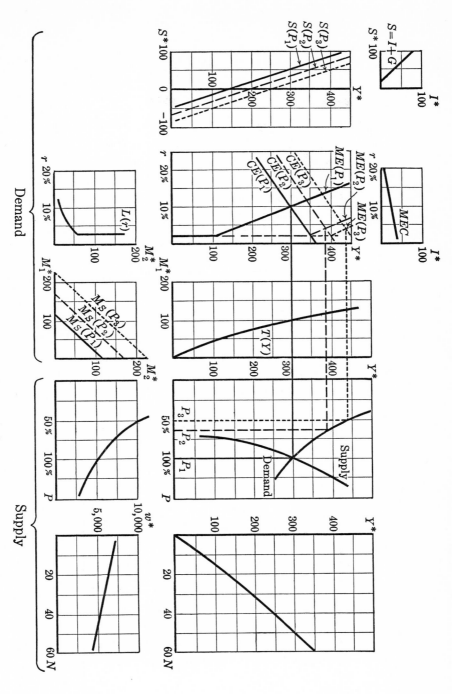

Fig. 36 Aggregate Demand and Supply and Their Components

DISCUSSION QUESTIONS

Would you expect an increase or a decrease in P, Y^*, N, I^*, and C^* to result from:

1. increased marginal efficiency of capital?
2. decreased money supply?
3. decreased money wages?
4. technological progress?
5. increased government spending?
6. rise in consumption function?

CHAPTER 15

Classical and Modern Analysis

JOHN MAYNARD KEYNES wrote *The General Theory of Employment, Interest and Money*, usually known as the *General Theory*, in 1936. In it he outlined the theory of income determination described in this volume. Some changes have been made since that time, but the general outlines are the same.

Much discussion has centered around the differences between this theory and the one that it replaced. This older theory is usually called the classical analysis. Many parts of it we now consider incorrect. Most of these errors are the result of changes in the world rather than of mistakes on the part of those who developed the theory. The nineteenth century was a period of rapid expansion in western Europe and the United States. It was also a period when the banking system was much less developed than now. In such circumstances, there was a sufficient supply of investment opportunities; the problem was to find funds to finance them. There were, therefore, no problems of determining the level of employment. All who wanted to work would be employed. Similarly, income was determined by production at full employment. The real wage was determined by competition in the labor market. As prices changed, the money wage changed proportionately. Only two problems remained: the determination of the price level, and the division of the national income between consumption and saving. (Actually there were depressions in this period, but the general tenor was so expansionary that they were passed off as unimportant and as the result of frictional elements in the society.)

Figure 37 shows the aggregate supply curve as visualized by the classical system. Since the money wage was the result of competitive bargaining, it could be ignored. Thus, the diagram has only three parts instead of the four parts used in Chapter 12. Note that the level of production is independent of the price level. Employment and the real wage are determined by the intersection of the labor supply and demand. Income is represented by possible production at this employment. To find the money wage, we use the definition

(1) $w = Pw^*.$

The money wage is the price level times the real wage.

The division of national income between investment and saving was believed to be determined by the interest rate. The demand for funds for investment is determined by productivity —what we have called the marginal efficiency of capital. The supply of funds came from saving. But what determines changes in saving? A concept such as the consumption function is useless, since income would be as high as it was possible to produce. If income did not change, one must look to other factors to influence saving. Foremost among these was the rate of interest. In Chapter 10, we mentioned that the rate of interest may have been an important determinant of saving at one time, even though we no longer consider it to be so. The intersection of the saving and investment schedules determined the rate of interest and the amount of saving and investment. This decision divides the national income between consumption and investment. This equilibrium is shown in graphic form in Figure 38.

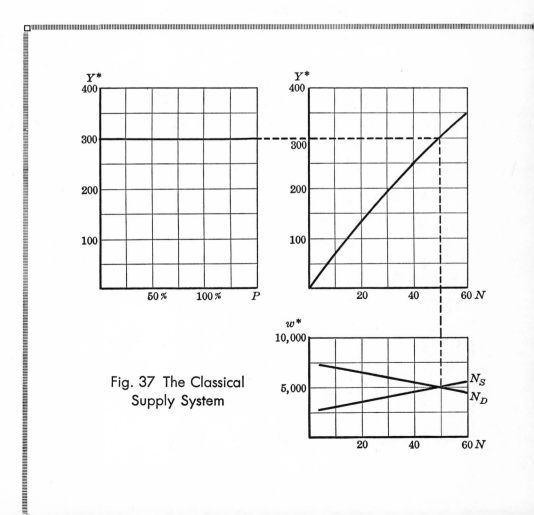

Fig. 37 The Classical
Supply System

There remains only the determination of the price level. In the simplest form, the price level depends upon the money supply. This is approximately the same as the transactions demand for money. Money must be used for transactions. The amount of money required depends upon the total number of transactions, the average price of each, and the number of times the money is used in a given period of time. The transactions, in turn, depend upon the level of national income and the organization of the economic process—how many hands goods pass through between original producer and final consumer. The relationship is summed up in the quantity equation

$$(2) \qquad\qquad\qquad MV = PT,$$

which assumes M to be the amount of money; V, the velocity or number of times it is spent per year; P, the price level; and T, the number of transactions. This equation is a mere definition,

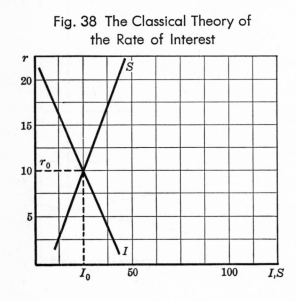

Fig. 38 The Classical Theory of the Rate of Interest

because V is defined so as to make this equation true, but it does serve to focus attention on these several factors. T is a direct function of the national income, which is determined by technical limitations. V depends upon the spending habits of the population.

This equation can be represented by the transactions demand for money. M_1^* depends upon total transactions, which depend upon income. This function is shown in Figure 39.

The slope of the curve in Figure 39 depends upon the size of V. The higher is V, the flatter will be the curve. Notice that the bottom scale is measured in two ways: in total value of transactions (at some basic price), and in total income. For the sake of simplicity, we have assumed that every dollar of income gives rise to three dollars of transactions. The equilibrium income, Y_0^*, is that given by Figure 37, the aggregate supply curve. From this curve, we can find the real value of money

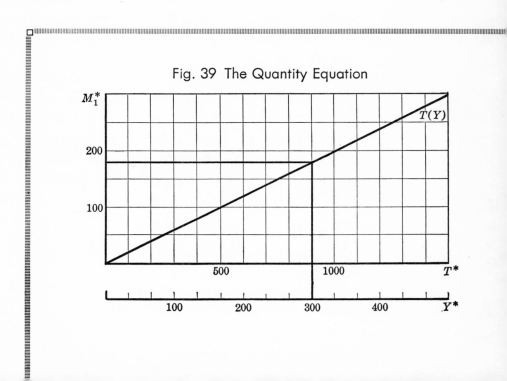

Fig. 39 The Quantity Equation

needed for transactions. Knowing this, we can find the price level by referring to the definition.

(3)
$$M* = \frac{M}{P}.$$

Multiplying both sides by P and dividing by $M*$, we find that

(4)
$$P = \frac{M}{M*}.$$

From this equation, we see that price changes proportionately with the money supply. This conclusion is called the *quantity theory*, here stated in its crudest form.

Except for this last part, the classical theory is very similar to the modern theory. The difference in the supply function can be explained by the growth of unions, which have given a special rigidity to the money wage. The reason for giving less attention to the rate of interest was discussed in Chapter 10. Only in the quantity theory is there any great difference from the modern theory.

The shift from the crude theory outlined above to the modern theory was a gradual one. One of the most important steps was the division of money into active and passive balances. Active balances are used currently for transactions; passive balances are used less frequently. This can be stated as a difference in velocity between the two types of balances. The revised quantity equation becomes

(4)

assuming M_1 and V_1 to be the active balances and their velocity, respectively, and M_2 and V_2 to be passive balances and their velocity. Most changes in price can be explained by shifts of money from active to passive and back. The description in Chapter 7 is an extreme form of this, in which M_2 is assumed to have a velocity of zero. The classical theory lacked a systematic explanation of the reason for shifts in M_2. In the Keynesian version, these are related to shifts in the interest rate. This change and the different description of aggregate supply are the principal elements of the Keynesian revolution. They introduced the possibility of an equilibrium position at less than full employment. Such a possibility did not exist in the classical version. In the classical system, income was fixed by technology and therefore could not affect saving by its variations. If income is considered a variable, the saving function was a natural extension.

These analytical differences between classical and modern theory do not indicate the psychological impact of Keynes upon economics. The possibility of unemployment equilibrium destroyed the faith in the perfection of the economic system. If full employment was not automatic, government interference might be necessary. Around this possibility, great political arguments arose, studded with varied epithets. This argument has now subsided; the victory has gone to Keynesian analysis, with modifications. This book has therefore been devoted to Keynesian tools, but the present chapter is intended to describe the previous theories, the indebtedness of Keynes to his predecessors, and the essential characteristics of his innovation. The bibliography to this chapter suggests additional discussions of the relationship.

DISCUSSION QUESTIONS

1. As technological progress makes greater production possible, would you expect the saving curve to remain fixed? If not, how would it change?

2. How would you alter Figure 38 to allow for the fact that the government and some consumers are borrowers and banks are lenders?

3. If all changes in prices are explained by movements between active and passive balances, of what use is the theory?

SUGGESTED ADDITIONAL READINGS

Discussions of Keynes and his predecessors are so numerous that only a modest selection can be given here. J. R. Hicks, "Mr. Keynes and the Classics," *Econometrica*, April 1937, reprinted in Bernard F. Haley (ed.), *Readings in the Theory of Income Distribution* (Philadelphia: Blakiston, 1944), presents one widely held interpretation. *The New Economics*, edited by Seymour E. Harris (New York: Knopf, 1950), contains several articles on the subject. Especially recommended are those by W. W. Leontief, R. F. Harrod, J. E. Meade, and Abba P. Lerner. Lawrence R. Klein discusses this relationship in Chapters 3, 4, and 5 of *The Keynesian Revolution* (New York: Macmillan, 1947). A. C. Pigou gives a somewhat rehabilitated version of the classical system in *Lapses from Full Employment* (London: Macmillan, 1945). Finally, Keynes himself emphasizes his differences from earlier theorists in *The General Theory of Employment, Interest and Money* (New York: Harcourt Brace, 1936), especially in Chapter 2 and the Appendix to Chapter 19. Those attempting to read Keynes himself will find much help in Alvin Hansen, *Guide to Keynes* (New York: McGraw-Hill, 1953).

CHAPTER 16

Theory and Practice

THE PURPOSE of this book has been to develop analytical tools for the study of national income and employment. Since tools are valuable only if they are used, this book should lead students to the discussion of questions of public policy. This final chapter is intended to serve as a warning against hasty and incomplete applications of the principles presented in previous chapters. In it, we shall discuss a few problems as examples of the kind of analysis required for policy decisions.

One should never lose sight of the limitations of any form of analysis. We have been discussing only the total figures for society and have ignored the changes that take place within these totals. For example, we have discussed only national income and have not considered the distribution of that income. Similarly, we have discussed taxes without considering the tax burden on individuals. Much of the public discussion accompanying any tax bill centers on these distributional aspects. Such discussion has a basis, both economic and ethical, not considered in this volume.

Another factor that we have neglected deals with the effects of time. In discussing aggregate demand, we mentioned that *rising* prices often have effects opposite to those of *higher* prices. In order to study changing conditions, we require a complete dynamic analysis with specification of the time lags that are appropriate. For example, it might be reasonable to give a consumption function relating consumption to last month's income.

The question of time is important also in analyzing political action. It is one thing to suggest that automatic forces will bring about recovery from a depression, but politicians facing re-election, and their constituents, may well feel that action is called for to speed up the process. During the relatively mild recession of 1953-54, for example, there was great disagreement among politicians over the proper course for the government to take. Should it let the recession run its course, or should it provide stimulus through varied governmental programs? In part, these debates stemmed from disagreement over the seriousness of the depression, but largely they were a measure of the patience of the politicians. In the end, the government adopted a policy of mild stimulus and allowed the automatic reactions to do the rest.

As soon as we enter the area of government activity, other problems arise. The role of value judgments is nowhere more obvious than in discussing government programs. Equally competent economists may disagree because they have different views on the ultimate goals toward which the society should work. As we shall see in a later section of this chapter, a nation with strong unions probably cannot have both full employment and stable prices. Some economists, thinking of those individuals who must live on fixed incomes, will prefer stable prices. Others, thinking of the hardships of unemployment, will prefer full employment. Economics offers no methods for determining that one of these preferences is right and the other wrong.

Some of these value judgments are quite widespread. In general, it is better to attain high-level employment without undue increase in government expenditures if this is possible. The reason for this preference is that government make-work projects are apt to be of less value to the society than similar expenditures made by individuals for themselves. Not all private spending has this advantage over government spending. Some investments that businesses might be encouraged to undertake are as inefficient or as useless as corresponding government projects. This is especially true of programs that are undertaken to comply with a government plan rather than as a regular profit-making activity. For this reason, it is not always true that the government should encourage business rather than undertake its own spending. Here again, people may disagree because they put different estimates on the value of government and business programs.

A final problem is raised by the size of the coefficients of some of our functions. If the multiplier is 10, it might be easy to persuade political leaders to restore full employment through government spending. In such a case, a gap of 50 billion dollars would require five billion of additional spending. If the multiplier is nearer two, it might be more difficult to persuade them to spend the required 25 billion dollars. Similarly, union leaders might consent to a 10-percent decline in money wages and prices to restore full employment but balk if the required decline were 90 percent. The size of these factors can be determined only by statistical analysis, some of it beyond the range of available data and methods.

All these cautions are not intended to imply that economic questions are unanswerable but rather to indicate that they are not trivial. The remaining sections of this chapter discuss certain problems to indicate the way in which various aspects of the previous analysis must be brought together to provide a solution.

TECHNOLOGICAL UNEMPLOYMENT

One of the most persistent debates in economics concerns the effect of technological change upon employment. In the early days of the Industrial Revolution, workers smashed machines in their fear that the machines would supplant them in their jobs. Eventually, however, it became clear that technological improvement did not lead to permanent unemployment, for new jobs would be found for the displaced workers. Karl Marx created a new spectre, that of the Reserve Army of the Unemployed. According to Marx, technological change always led to temporary unemployment, and, before the displaced workers could be absorbed, new workers would be displaced by new machines.

Thus, there would always be some members of society who were technologically unemployed.

In a superficial sense, Marx's view is correct. At any time, there are always some workers between jobs and therefore unemployed. Marx claimed more than this, however, for he felt that the reserve army kept wages down. For this to be true, it is necessary that the number of unemployed workers should exceed

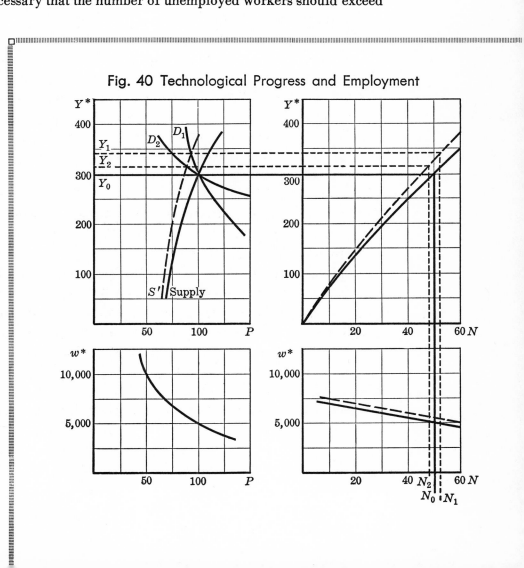

Fig. 40 Technological Progress and Employment

the number of unfilled jobs. We shall apply the analysis of this volume in considering this problem. For simplicity, we shall assume that the supply of labor is fixed. The question then can be restated thus: "If a society starts from a position of full employment, will technological improvement increase or decrease the amount of labor demanded?" It is the demand for labor that affects the level of wages.

The analysis of this problem requires mainly the tools of aggregate supply. Technological change is represented by an upward shift of the production function. Ordinarily, such a shift also means a similar movement of the marginal productivity curve. The result of these changes is a new aggregate supply curve, shown in Figure 40.

Figure 40 shows us that, at every level of prices, more output would be offered than previously. Similarly, we see that no matter what the shape of the demand curve, the real income will rise. If the demand curve is relatively elastic (like D_1), there will be a large change in output and a slight change in prices. If the demand is inelastic (like D_2), the change will be more in prices and less in output.

What of the demand for labor? Any given output can now be produced with less labor than before. We would therefore expect that a slight increase in output would result in fewer jobs and that a large increase in output would result in more jobs. Figure 40 shows this to be the case: with the elastic demand, D_1, employment increases from N_0 to N_1; with the inelastic demand, D_2, employment falls to N_2.

We could have arrived at the same conclusion from a consideration of the price. With the new higher marginal product curve, employers would hire more workers at each real wage. However, the price decline associated with technological change has the effect of raising real wages. If the price change is small, the shift of the productivity curve will outweigh the rise in real wages; if the price change is large, the rise in wages will be more important.

Technological change may also shift the marginal efficiency of capital, usually upward. If so, the demand curve also shifts up, making an increase in employment more probable.

We find then that there is no absolute answer to the problem of technological unemployment. If the demand is elastic, the total number of jobs will increase, and workers can be sure that anyone who loses his job will find another waiting for him. If demand is inelastic, technological change may require downward adjustment of money wages. In such a case, Marx would be right. Whether the aggregate demand will be elastic or inelastic will vary from country to country and time to time. Consumers and investors, by their preferences for lower prices or more goods, determine the effects of technology upon employment. When Marx announced the reserve army as a general law, he was quite wrong. Had he mentioned it as a possibility, he would have been correct.

THE UNEASY TRIANGLE

Not all the problems of aggregate economic analysis deal with unemployment. Many problems are raised by a full-employment society, especially if the full employment is the result of government action. In the United States, the Employment Act of 1946 states that it is the responsibility of the government to maintain a high and stable level of employment. Some doubt has arisen as to whether it is possible to maintain such an employment level without having continually rising prices. The basis of this doubt is the strength of American labor unions. Many people feel that unions will be able to force a continued increase in money wages if there is little unemployment. If money wages rise, the government will be able to guarantee either full employment or stable prices but not both. For this reason, wages, employment, and prices are sometimes known as the uneasy triangle.

It is beyond the limits of this volume to investigate whether unions can actually succeed in raising wages. For purposes of the argument, let us assume that they can. We represent this increase by a new line in Part A of Figure 29. The new supply curve will indicate lower production at each price level, as shown in Figure 41.

The income of Y_0^* is assumed to be an initial starting point of full employment. If aggregate demand remains the same, income would fall to Y_1^* and prices would rise to P_1. The government has certain powers to control aggregate demand. It can either increase or decrease demand. By increasing demand to D_1, the government could maintain full employment and an income Y_0^*, but only at the cost of a higher price level, P_2. The original price could be maintained only by decreasing demand to D_2, but such a decrease would lead to lower income and employment.

The only hope for stability lies in technological progress. We saw in the preceding section of this chapter that such a change would move the supply curve in the opposite direction. A move back to the original position, S, would not be enough, for an income of Y_0* would not mean full employment if the production function shifts. Only a shift in supply beyond the original level is sufficient to bring about full employment with-

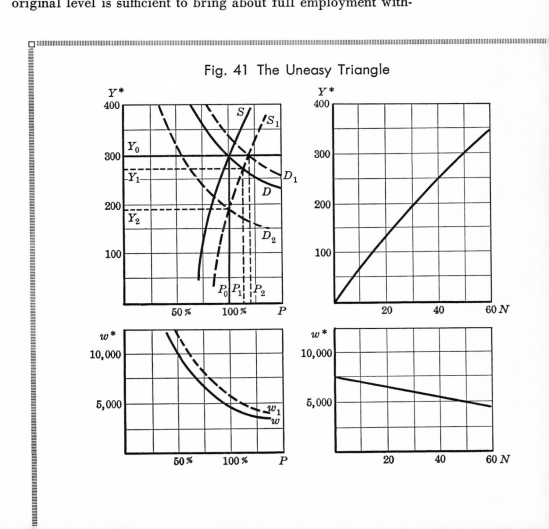

Fig. 41 The Uneasy Triangle

out an increase in prices. Even in this case, some increase in demand may be necessary, for, as we saw in the preceding pages, technological change decreases employment if the demand curve is inelastic.

Thus, the only way in which to maintain full employment and stable prices with a rising money wage is for productivity to increase even faster. Whether productivity will win this race only time will tell.

GOVERNMENT SPENDING AND TAXES

In Chapter 4 we discussed the relative effects of government spending and taxes upon national income. Our analysis discussed only the multipliers—that is, the reaction of consumption to the change in government activity. In Chapter 9, we noted that investment also is affected by government spending and taxes. In order to find the complete result of a change in government fiscal activities, it is necessary to combine the direct multiplier effects with the multiplier effects of the induced investment. In such a case, the total change in income is expressed by

(1) $$\Delta Y = k_G \Delta G + k_I \Delta I \text{ and}$$

(2) $$\Delta Y = k_{Tx} \Delta Tx + k_I \Delta I.$$

Let us consider an example of such changes. If the marginal propensity to consume is two-thirds, what would be the effects of a change of five billion dollars in government spending and taxes? The simple multipliers indicate a change of 10 billion dollars from the tax changes and 15 billion dollars from the government spending. (The government-spending multiplier is three; the tax multiplier is two.)

It is quite possible that the change in investment that results from a tax change is more than that resulting from government spending. The reason, of course, is that potential taxes may affect investment just as much as the taxes actually collected. For purposes of our example, let us assume that each dollar of government spending increases investment by 10 cents but that each dollar of tax cut increases investment by 50 cents. In such a case, the total expansion from a five-billion-dollar increase in government spending is 16.5 billion dollars. Using equation 1 and substituting values, we find that

(1) $$\Delta Y = k_G \Delta G + k_I \Delta I;$$

(3) $$\Delta Y = 3 \times \$5 + 3 \times \$.5$$
$$= \$15 + \$1.5$$
$$= \$16.5.$$

Using equation 2, we find that the expansion from a five-billion-dollar tax cut is 17.5 billion dollars:

(2) $$\Delta Y = k_{Tx} \Delta Tx + k_I \Delta I;$$

(4) $$\Delta Y = (-2) \times (-\$5) + 3 \times \$2.5$$
$$= \$10 + \$7.5$$
$$= \$17.5.$$

In such a circumstance, the balanced-budget multiplier might actually be negative—that is, a larger budget might mean a smaller national income. In the example above, an increase in government spending of five billion dollars would increase national income by 16.5 billion dollars whereas a tax increase of the same amount would decrease income by 17.5 billion dollars. An equal *increase* of five billion dollars in both government spending and taxes would therefore *reduce* national income by one billion dollars.

The practical importance of this result depends upon many factors. In a depression, there is apt to be excess capacity in many lines of business. In such circumstances, one should expect only slight changes in investment. The total income change is then only the direct multiplier effect. In periods of generally high-level activity, one might expect substantial investment reaction, along the lines given above. For this reason, tax changes are usually considered better methods of fighting inflation and slight recessions, but government spending is more effective against a real depression.

Another factor that we have neglected in analyzing government activities is the effect on the money market of government financing techniques. If the government finances its deficits by borrowing from individuals, the total money supply is unchanged. If it prints money, the money supply expands by the amount of the deficit. If the government borrows from the banks, the money supply may increase by a multiple of the deficit as a result of bank-deposit creation. If these expansionary methods of financing are chosen, one must make the appropriate changes in the money equilibrium curve as well as in the commodity equilibrium curve. In general, a government deficit financed by bank borrowing is more expansionary than the same program financed by borrowing from individuals, unless the interest rate is already at the minimal level. If this minimum has been achieved, no change in the money market affects the level of national income.

CONCLUSION

Throughout this book, we have been discussing tools that will help us to solve questions of public policy. Any such solutions have three ingredients: value judgments, empirical facts, and analytical tools. The value judgments tell us what goals we seek. As such, they are beyond the reach of economics and are the province of religion and philosophy. The empirical facts are necessary for decision but are subject to rapid change. Many agencies of the government and some of the large private research organizations are engaged in preparing such information. The analytical tools, with which this book has been mainly concerned, tell us how to manipulate facts to find techniques for attaining the desired goals. These three elements are interwoven in the solution of any actual problem. In this volume, we have tried to keep them as distinct as possible, for the sake of clarity. This separation also has another advantage. Most disagreements between economists are the result of differences in goals or in estimates of facts. A complete understanding of analysis does not solve any economic problem, but it is an indispensable tool with which to begin the solution.

Index